Daniel C. Eddy

Our Travelling Party in Ireland

Daniel C. Eddy

Our Travelling Party in Ireland

ISBN/EAN: 9783743317086

Manufactured in Europe, USA, Canada, Australia, Japa

Cover: Foto ©ninafisch / pixelio.de

Manufactured and distributed by brebook publishing software (www.brebook.com)

Daniel C. Eddy

Our Travelling Party in Ireland

OUR TRAVELLING PARTY

IN

IRELAND.

BY
DANIEL C. EDDY.

ILLUSTRATED.

BOSTON:
D. LOTHROP & COMPANY,
FRANKLIN ST., CORNER HAWLEY.

PREFACE.

This volume commences a series of books for youth, adapted to please, instruct, and benefit. The aim will be to give the youthful reader a clear, accurate account of foreign scenes and society. Every effort will be made to make the statements reliable, and the books permanently useful, not merely to the young, but to all persons whose circumstances will not allow them to go abroad.

The author proposes to follow a travelling party through the principal countries of Europe, into Egypt, Palestine, and Greece. Though the successive volumes will be connected in name and style, and will be issued as a serial, a few months intervening between them, each one will be complete in itself.

These books will be sent out into a field that never can be filled, for the children's department of our literature makes constant demands, and every volume published for young persons only creates a taste that calls for others; and this series is given to the public with the hope that each successive volume may prove useful, instructive, and entertaining. The next volume, which will soon be issued, will take the traveller through Scotland and England.

CONTENTS.

CHAP.		PAGE
I.	The Percy Mansion.	11
II.	The Atlantic Voyage.	29
III.	Glimpses of Liverpool.	53
IV.	A Walk on Chester Walls.	77
V.	A Ride through North Wales.	101
VI.	Crossing the Channel.	112
VII.	The Irish Capital.	119
VIII.	Fancy Trip to Cork.	148
IX.	Visit to the Lakes of Killarney.	176
X.	Maynooth and Drogheda.	192
XI.	Glances at Giant's Causeway.	206
XII.	Dunluce Castle.	218
XIII.	A Day in Belfast.	225
XIV.	Farewell to Ireland.	239

ENGRAVINGS.

	PAGE
GOLDEN CROSS ABBEY.	2
THE PERCY MANSION.	10
STEAMER NIAGARA.	47
WALTER'S TIME TABLE.	76
GOD'S PROVIDENCE HOUSE.	91
BRITANNIA BRIDGE.	105
SHANDON STEEPLE.	155
BLARNEY CASTLE.	171
IRISH RIDING.	189
AN IRISH TOWN.	197
GIANT'S WELL AND GUIDE.	207
GIANT'S GATEWAY.	210

THE PERCY MANSION.

THE PERCY FAMILY.

Chapter I.

THE PERCY MANSION.

IN the beautiful city of Cambridge, near Boston, stands the aristocratic mansion of Peter Percy, Esq., a rich merchant, who has long been engaged in the West India trade, and who has accumulated a vast fortune, by prudence, economy, skill, and sound judgment. The Percy family consists of the father, mother, and three lovely children of the respective ages of eleven, nine, and six. The oldest, Walter, is a thoughtful, sedate, studious boy, who never gave his parents a moment's uneasiness, and who is a patient devotee of books. Intellect is written on his fair brow, his pale features are stamped with genius, and already he shows the dawnings of that light which will make him a bright example. The second child is Minnie, the antipode of Walter, a mild, beautiful girl, whose brown hair falls in wavy ringlets on her shoulders, and whose sunny smile is the light of the house and the joy of the home circle. Impatient and nervous, she would rather gather buttercups and daisies than pore over books; healthful and cheerful, she turns every thing upside down, answering the remonstrance of her mother with a merry laugh that is irresistible, and that drives every frown from that look of maternal love. Every body loves Minnie Percy, and she is justly the pride of her parents. Charlie is the youngest, a noble boy, of good proportions and fair appearance, who has yet to develop himself in order to have his traits of character fully seen. The family, when together, is one of the most happy in the place; no cloud rests upon their home, which is one of great magnificence.

Peter Percy himself is a man of intelligence, reading, and business sagacity; a devout Christian, and a man deeply interested in every good enterprise, and every philanthropic movement, liberal to the poor, just to himself, and grateful to God.

One evening this merchant returned to his mansion, and, after tea had been served, and the gas lighted, called his family together, and told them that he was about to leave the cares and anxieties of business for a while, and seek recreation and rest in a foreign tour. Walter's large, dreamy eyes were at once fixed on his father's face, and little Minnie clapped her hands for joy.

"Will you take me?" said Walter.

"I will go," enthusiastically cried Minnie, almost breathless with impetuosity.

"And me too, pa!" chimed in Charlie.

"Stop, children," said Mr. Percy, "and let us talk over this matter. Perhaps mamma will have a word to say about it."

Mrs. Percy, who had previously been made acquainted with her husband's plans, smiled upon her lovely children, as, with one accord, the trio appealed to her.

"May we go, mamma?"

"I cannot spare you all. Who would come and kiss mamma in the morning?"

"I will stay at home with mamma," said Charlie, half in sorrow. "I do not want to go away with papa; I will stay at home with mamma."

A kiss was the only answer the mother gave as she touched the brow of her fair child, from which the sunny hair was thrown back. The little fellow looked up as he felt a tear drop on his cheek, and added,—

"Shall not Charlie have a rocking horse if he stays at home?"

The promise having been made that Charlie should have his rocking horse, and that Walter and Minnie should accompany Mr. Percy on his European tour, the evening was spent in making arrangements, and talking over plans for the future, until the time came for sleep, when the whole family, after seeking direction and counsel of God, the great Father, retired to rest. But Walter and Minnie could not sleep much. Their little heads were side by side, and long, in low whispers, did they converse of the things they expected to see on their arrival in Europe; and it was after midnight when sleep overpowered them.

The sun had scarcely risen the next morning ere the children were all up; and a more merry family circle one would not desire to see, than that which gathered around Mr. Percy's table that day. The children were happy in the idea of seeing so many different lands, and so many strange scenes. Walter had read of London and Rome, and Minnie had often heard of Paris, the gay and beautiful metropolis of fashion, and the prospect of seeing those places took away all inclination to study, or even eat. Breakfast being over, the family carriage, a vehicle of more utility than beauty, of more real comfort than elegance of appearance, was brought to the door by the servant, and Mr. Percy, addressing his son, said, —

"Come, Walter, get ready and we will go into the city and purchase our tickets, and secure our berths for the voyage."

"What, father, so soon as this?"

"Yes, my son; at this season of the year the steamers are so crowded that passage must be taken several weeks in advance."

On the way to the city, Mr. Percy explained more fully his plans to his son, and gave him an outline of the route he proposed to take. Walter had studied geography carefully, and had read history somewhat extensively, and was acquainted with many of the cities which had been marked down as worthy of a visit, and the conversation on these places gave evidence that the lad had made much proficiency in his studies, and could appreciate the voyage he was about to make. Many men of means travel, but acquire no information, and fail of enlarging their minds, because they are strangers to the historical importance of the places they visit; and Mr. Percy was well pleased that his son should develop so much knowledge of the places of historic interest, and sacred to the memory of heroes and martyrs. He found that the lad was to be a better travelling companion than some men of mature years, but of less observation and reading, could possibly be.

To travel well, a man must be a genius — he must have an aptitude for travelling. Some men may go around the world and never see any thing, or become any wiser for the pains they take to visit distant lands. They have no genius for travelling. They go with their eyes shut, their ears closed, and their hearts sealed. They will ride through an enchanting country, reading some romance, or poring over the last political article in the London Times. They visit cities, but they never get any knowledge of the customs of the people. They are not gifted with the faculty for travelling, and might as well stay at home.

It was not so with our young hero. He was observant of every thing that passed before him, and before he had secured his passage, he had laid out his plans, and, in imagination, lived over half his journey.

"Here we are at the booking office," said Mr. Percy, as he reined up his horse in front of a noble edifice on State Street; and the two went up stairs into the office of the agent, and Mr. Percy inquired of that gentleman, —

"What steamer sails two weeks from to-day?"

"The Niagara, sir."

"Who will command her on the passage?"

"Captain Wickman, one of the best officers in the service."

"Is she full?"

"Nearly so, but a few state rooms yet remain unengaged."

"Will you show me the plan?"

"Certainly, sir, with the greatest pleasure."

Mr. Percy looked over the plan, and found that state rooms, with berths, numbered 71 and 72, were not taken, and at once engaged them, and having also secured a berth for Minnie, in the state room for ladies, gave his check on the Boylston Bank for the amount. All this time Walter stood looking on, and wondering how large the room could be, and what kind of a berth he should have, and was aroused from his reflections by the question of the agent, —

"Would you not like to take your son over to the dock at East Boston, and let him see the steamer?"

"Well, what say, Walter?" asked Mr. Percy.

"O, by all means, let us go over," was the reply.

The agent furnished Mr. Percy with a ticket,

and entering the carriage, the father and son drove rapidly to the ferry. The boat was just starting, and they had barely time to get aboard before the bell rang, and the huge, unwieldy float moved out into the channel; and in a few minutes a dull, heavy crash announced the arrival at East Boston. Driving to the steamer landing, and showing the ticket to the gate tender, they were allowed to go on deck, and see the vessel which was to bear them across the deep. They found their state room to be a very pleasant one, but in a state of confusion, as the steamer was being cleansed for her trip. The servants, however, were very polite, and the steward asked Mr. Percy if he would not select seats at the table, as it might be too late when he came aboard again. So they went into the magnificent saloon, and found several long tables, and Mr. Percy, turning to his son, said, —

"Walter, where would you like to sit?"

Walter looked along the table, and replied, "I would like to sit near the captain, so that we may have the benefit of his conversation."

"That," said the steward, pointing to a table near the door, "is the captain's table; but five seats are already taken there. The next table is not taken."

So seats were selected at the second table,

and Walter, writing his father's name on one card, and his own on another, handed them to the steward, who said the seats should be reserved.

After looking about the steamer, going into both cabins, examining the huge engine,—which now was silent and still, like a great dead thing, incapable of motion,—and talking with the officers and men, our friends, whom we have accompanied to the steamer, took their carriage and leisurely rode back to the city, through Charlestown, not crossing the ferry as they had done before. They reached the city just as the sun was setting, and stopping for a moment at his counting house, Mr. Percy then drove rapidly to his house in Cambridge. Minnie was waiting for them with the greatest impatience, and before they had time to enter the house, she cried, " Have you got the tickets, Walter? Did you see the steamer, father? Will any ladies go over with us? When shall we start?"

" Stop, stop, my dear; one question at a time, my child," said Mr. Percy, in a tone savoring of slight rebuke. " You must learn to be patient;" and then, with a pleasant smile, added, " I will let Walter answer your questions while I go and see that the carriage is taken care of."

"I will tell you all about it after tea," said Walter.

"After tea, indeed! I must hear about it now."

"Well, I will tell you all I know." So Walter sat down with his sister, and told her all that had been done, and described the vessel, and the state room, and the appearance of the captain, and detailed much of the conversation which had occurred between him and his father, all of which interested the little girl very much.

"And now, father, what else have we to do before we go?" said Walter, as the family were seated at the tea table.

"O, several things," was the reply. "We have to purchase some nice new trunks and carpet bags; we have to secure our passports, and mamma has much work to do to get us all ready. We shall want a few letters of introduction to distinguished persons, whom we must try to see, but on whom it would not be courteous to call without an introduction. We must get a letter of credit, so that, when we are in want of money, we can go to the bankers in London, Paris, Vienna, or Rome, and draw as much as we need. And several other little things must be attended to ere we shall be ready to sail."

THE PERCY MANSION. 21

"What is a letter of credit?" asked Walter.

"What is a passport?" asked Minnie.

"I will answer Walter's question first, as it was asked first. A letter of credit is a banking document, which is taken from a banker in Boston, who has correspondence with bankers in all the prominent European cities. I deposit with the banker here a sum of money, or my note for a certain amount, and receive the letter in return. When I want money in Paris or Naples, I take the letter to a banker, whose name is on this paper, and he gives me fifty or a hundred dollars, just as I may want. By this arrangement, I am not obliged to carry gold, which would be very heavy, and would be a source of continual anxiety. Do you understand?"

"I think I do."

"Well, I will explain it more fully to you when we draw money in some foreign city."

"And now my question," said Minnie. "What is a passport?"

"A passport, my child, is a document given by the secretary of state, at Washington, showing that I am an American citizen. So, when I go into any country, the police will know who I am, and not confound me with those who are trying to overthrow the government. In this country and in England, passports are not required, but all over the continent they are demanded."

"But if you should not have one, what would be the result?" asked Minnie.

"Why, when we reached the French frontier, we should be sent back or arrested."

"O, that would be funny."

"More perplexing than funny, my child."

"And what should we do?"

"Well, we might go to London and get a passport from Mr. Dallas, the American minister, as he has power to give it. But we could not travel without it any where upon the continent."

Thus conversing, the tea hour passed away, the evening advanced, and the hour for family devotions having arrived, the whole family bowed before the great Father, sought his protection, and separated for the night.

The next morning Mr. Percy and Walter rode into Boston, and, calling at the Custom House, made an arrangement with a polite official for a passport. Walter and his father were measured, their ages taken, and a general description of them made. This description was sent to Washington, and a few days elapsed before the document was received. They then went to the banker, and made arrangements with him for a letter of credit, Mr. Percy putting a large sum of money on deposit, and receiving the necessary document. They then went to a trunk maker, and bought two stout trunks, and two fine carpet bags. They next repaired to a clothing store, where a nice suit of gray travelling clothes were bought for Walter, a loose drab sack for Mr. Percy, and one or two articles for Minnie. All this, with some business matters not connected with the tour, occupied most of the day, and they returned in the afternoon, again to be overwhelmed with questions by Minnie, who in the mean while had been busy with her mother in preparing her clothes, and getting ready for the voyage.

After a few days Mr. Percy received a large document, bearing the seal of the United States, and on opening it, it was found to be the passports for the travellers; and as many of our readers may never have seen a passport, we give a copy of one on the next page, as nearly as we can in so small a space.

Day by day the arrangements progressed, and soon the trio were all ready to start; and as the time approached, the young folks became more anxious to be on the way. The steamer was to start on the seventh day of April, and the hours and minutes to that time were counted and wished away. However, none of the time was

UNITED STATES OF AMERICA.

To all to whom these Presents shall come, greeting:

No. 6831.

DESCRIPTION.

STATURE, 5 FT. 8 INCH.
AGE, 35 YEARS.
FOREHEAD, HIGH.
EYES, GRAY.
NOSE, SMALL.
MOUTH, MEDIUM.
CHIN, ROUND.
HAIR, BROWN.
COMPLEXION, LIGHT.
FACE, MEDIUM.

The undersigned, Secretary of State of the United States of America, hereby requests all whom it may concern, to permit safely and freely to pass *Peter Percy,* a citizen of the United States, and in case of need to give him all useful aid and protection.

Given under my hand and the impression of the Seal of the Department of State, at the City of Washington, the 29th day of March, A. D. 1858, in the 82d year of the Independence of the United States.

Lewis Cass.

Signature of Bearer.

Peter Percy.

U. S. Seal.

lost to Walter, who busied himself in reading works of travel, and studying French phrases, and otherwise preparing himself to make the most of his tour.

On Saturday, before the time for sailing, just as the family were rising from the tea table, Mr. Tenant, one of Mr. Percy's most esteemed neighbors, called in, and, after the usual friendly salutations, said, " Friend Percy, I have come in to see if you want a companion on your tour. I have made up my mind to travel a few months, and should like to go abroad with you."

Mr. Percy gladly accepted the proposition, for Mr. Tenant was an enterprising business man, who would make a most excellent travelling companion. So it was arranged that Mr. Tenant, who had already engaged his passage, should make one of the party.

The steamer was to sail on Wednesday, and on the previous evening, Mr. Percy was sitting with his family in his spacious drawing room. There were present, besides the family, two maiden sisters of Mrs. Percy, who were to keep her company during the absence of her husband; and they were discussing, with some tinge of sadness, the events liable and likely to transpire during the summer. It was the last evening they would be together for a long time perhaps it would be the last time they would thus gather on earth. While they conversed and committed themselves to the protection of God, the bell rang, and a neighbor was ushered into the room; soon came another, and then another, and still others, until the rooms were crowded, and the house full of friends and neighbors, who had come in to give the Percys a happy surprise. Among them were professors and students of the college, men of wealth and refinement, and the pastor and deacons of the church with which the family worshipped. The brisk hands of the ladies soon spread a table in the dining room, and, after an hour had been spent in social converse, the whole company were invited to it, and full justice was done to the rich viands beneath which the table groaned. When the repast was nearly finished, and all were in a merry mood, a gentleman approached Mr. Percy, and thus addressed him: —

"Dear friend: We have come in to-night to wish you a happy voyage and a safe return; we have often enjoyed your kindness and hospitality, and we wished, in some slight way, to make you the recipient of ours. Will you please accept this cane, [handing Mr. Percy a magnificent cane, gold mounted,] manufactured from wood cut on the grounds of Mount Vernon, and finished with much taste by an artisan of the metropolis? It will remind you, when in distant lands, of the friends who, at home, will send up their daily prayers to the God of ocean and land for your protection. May your whole tour be pleasant, profitable, and safe; and may you return to your home, and to your business, with an invigorated step and renewed health, and long live, a blessing to your family and the world."

Mr. Percy made an appropriate reply, touching gratefully upon the pleasant relations which had always existed between him and his neighbors, and the pleasure he felt in seeing them in his drawing room that night, under such circumstances.

The ladies then placed in the hands of Mrs. Percy a beautiful bouquet, with the delicately expressed hope and wish, that when the flowers had faded, her cheek might bloom more beautifully, and that the fragrance of her example might still continue to be a blessing to the world.

The company remained together until ten o'clock, and then cordially shaking hands with the happy family, they departed, more than one lip uttering the precious sentence, "God bless them;" while the family soon sought repose, to dream, perchance, of the morrow and its scenes.

And those dreams were sweet, for conscience came with no upbraidings and reproaches to any who were beneath that roof that night. The wicked only dream of retribution; and they who love God and keep his commandments, rest in peace, as it is written, " He giveth his beloved sleep."

Chapter II.

THE ATLANTIC VOYAGE.

THE morning sun rose beautifully from its eastern bed; but long before it was seen, Walter and Minnie had been up, and made all their arrangements to drive into the city. The trunks, which had been packed the evening before, had been strapped by the servant upon the rack of the carriage, and the children were all ready. We need not speak of the sadness which came unbidden as that family sat down to the table; nor of the tender interview between the husband and wife, which, in the study, followed it; nor of the warm tears that fell upon the cheeks of the children as their mother folded them to her heart. The holy scene which is witnessed when a mother separates from her children, the pen had better not describe; for the bleeding heart and the gentle tears cannot be transferred to paper.

The plan was arranged for Mrs. Percy and Charlie to go into the city, and see the steamer start; and after breakfast the parents in one carriage, and the children in another, drove rapidly to Boston, and soon the whole company was assembled on the deck of the noble steamship Niagara. There all was orderly confusion.

Crowds of people, who had come down to see friends start off, thronged every part of the ship; baggage was being brought on by hurrying, driving, shouting porters; the officers of the ship moved about, giving their orders quietly. Among those assembled were many friends of the Percy family, and one of them, Mr. Cushman, put into the hands of Walter a beautiful spyglass, and handed to Minnie a neat pocket compass, both of which he said would be of service ere the party returned; and they were found to be so. Mr. Tenant was on hand in season, and at noon the bell warned all who were to land to do so at once; and Mrs. Percy. bidding her husband and children farewell, was assisted to the wharf by Mr. Cushman. The steamer soon left her moorings, and swung out into the harbor. A mighty cheer went up from the people on the land, answered by one as mighty from those on shipboard; a waving of handkerchiefs followed on both sides; a gun was fired on shipboard, repeated quickly, and in gallant style the noble vessel went down the harbor, and soon the people on land lost sight of her entirely.

For a long time, Mr. Percy and his children stood on deck, gazing back upon the fading spires and chimneys of the city, happy and yet sad. Walter was silent, noting every thing he saw, watching every object, and laying up in his memory every little circumstance. Minnie's tongue kept moving; she had a hundred questions to ask, and a hundred things to say. In two hours she had formed a dozen acquaintances, and drawn out towards her a dozen loving hearts. Her free, joyous spirit seemed to have lost restraint, and become lawless as the ocean. Thus time passed on, until all were aroused by a new sound.

"Ding, dong, ding — ding, dong, ding."

"What is that for, pa?" said Minnie.

"Why, dinner, Min — don't you know?" replied Walter, who wished to have it known that he was posted.

"Yes, it is dinner hour; four o'clock; eight bells, as the sailors say. And see, the passengers are going down, and we will go down with them."

The party went into the beautiful saloon, and our friends found their places at the table without difficulty. There were two rows of tables, each seating eight persons; and soon all were filled. At the first table was a gentleman, who, with his family, was going abroad to remain some months, and Minnie had already made the acquaintance of the young ladies. At the same table with themselves were two travellers from Iowa, a physician from Alabama, and two gentlemen from Boston, who very soon formed a strong mutual attachment. The dinner was highly relished, and Minnie, who ate nothing for breakfast, and had taken no lunch, declared it to be the best meal she had ever tasted. She partook of every thing, from the soup to the dessert, and, like the rest of the people, tarried an hour at the table. To Walter and Minnie, who had seldom been away from home, and who had never dined at a hotel or in a steamer, the whole scene was novel. The crash of table ware, the clatter of knives and forks, the call for wine and other liquors, the pleasant jokes, the general hilarity of the company, were very exciting to our young voyagers.

"Do you expect to dine with us to-morrow?" said the doctor to Minnie.

"Certainly, sir; why not?"

"Perhaps you will; but I think many who are here now will not be here to-morrow."

"Why not, sir; please tell me."

"Because to-morrow it will probably be very rough, and many will be seasick. I have crossed the ocean once or twice, and I never knew the tables to be very full on the second day."

"O, I shall not be seasick — I don't mean to be."

A merry laugh answered this expression of determination not to be seasick, and the company rose and went up on deck. Then it was found that the wind had changed, the sky was overcast, and a fog was beginning to settle over the vessel's course.

"A rough night we shall have," said one.

"If the fog only keeps off, we shall do well enough," added another.

Just then the vessel pitched so as to send Minnie half way across the deck. She recovered her position, but the quick eye of Mr. Percy detected a pallor on her countenance that he knew indicated seasickness, and he advised her to retire to her state room, and lie down a while.

"No, father; Walter would laugh at me."

"Ah, Min, you are seasick already."

Minnie rested her head a while on her father's knee, and then said, "I will go down; please assist me."

Mr. Percy led her to her room, and calling

the stewardess, bade her attend to the wants of the child, and again started for the deck. But on the way he met Walter staggering down, no better off than Minnie. His father assisted him to his berth, helped him to undress, and left him to himself. The night proved a dark and stormy one; the following day was rainy, and the east wind blew fiercely. Walter and Minnie both kept their berths, and Mr. Percy, as the steward said, was somewhat "under the weather." As the doctor had said, few were at the table, and those who were able to be there indulged in pleasantries and jokes at the expense of those who were not.

On Friday morning the steamer reached Halifax, and the children, feeling better as they neared port, were early on deck. The beautiful scenery drew the attention of all, and the interest increased as the ship neared the wharf, where she was to lie two hours to take in coal and provisions. Mr. Percy took the children, and, accompanied by Mr. Tenant, went up into the city, and after returning to the steamer, told Walter that he might send a line to his mother, if he would write quickly, as he himself was about to write, and could enclose a note from the children. We will give Walter's letter to his mother: —

Ever Dear Mother: —

We are at Halifax, in the dominions of the queen, and resting here for a short time gives me the opportunity of sending a line back to my dear, dear home, from which it seems a long time that I have been absent. I must be short, and tell you briefly what I have seen and felt thus far. I think it is John Kitto who says, in one of his letters, "To *have travelled* is a very fine thing, but it is *not* a very fine thing *to travel.*" With John Kitto I have just at this time a delightful fellow-feeling. John must have crossed the Atlantic Ocean, been shut up in a little state room in one of the British steamers, homesick, seasick, no appetite, no sleep, unable to read, pitching about, not knowing how soon the poor flesh will be the food of his majesty the sea serpent, and the bones lie whitening in the coral caves far down below. This is what men call "*being travelled.*" And this liquid earthquake, on which we have been reeling and rocking, tumbling and pitching, puffing and paddling, for days, is what poets and orators call

"The broad and beautiful sea."

Well, it is beautiful. It is intensely sublime. God marches on the deep; his form, sublime, sweeps along in his misty chariot, and his great, awful voice echoes from land to land. Even the godless Byron sees a God in the ocean. As he gazes upon the watery deep, it becomes

> "A glorious mirror, where the Almighty's form
> Glasses itself in tempests."

We started from Boston, as you know, on a very beautiful day, and had a very fine run out to sea, passing Deer Island, and the frowning fort on George's Island, and leaving the city, with its dear associations, and dearer friends, far behind. But gathering night brought with it an east wind, a dense fog, plenty of seasickness, and the usual annoyances of a sea voyage.

I can stand almost any thing but seasickness. This is the third day I have been out, and not an hour's exemption have I yet had from the gripe of his oceanic majesty. No one gets any sympathy for seasickness; there is no medicine to cure. Minnie and I have suffered much, and the steward is very kind. I think father has been sick, but he will not admit it. But I know you will smile, and say, "It is nothing but seasickness, and they will soon get over that, and be better for it afterwards;" so it is no use for me to write about that.

THE ATLANTIC VOYAGE. 37

We arrived at Halifax on Friday morning, and at once drew up to the wharf. Having two hours to stop, we went up into the city. The people were asleep, and all was as silent as a city of the dead. Our own tramp on the hard ground, our own voices ringing on the still air, alone disturbed the general quiet. That part of the city we saw was the worst part of Halifax, the better portions, which are said to be more beautiful, lying back on the hills. Halifax does not seem to have the thrift of a New England town, and that part visited by us, which was near the wharf, seemed to be a century behind the times. No paved thoroughfare, no brick sidewalk, no signs of recent improvement greeted the eye in any direction we went. The houses are generally small, built of wood, shingled roof and sides, and uncomely in their appearance. On the hill-side overlooking the city frowns a formidable fortification, which looks as if able to pour its deadly fires with murderous effect upon any hostile fleet that might venture into the waters below.

Father suggests to me that, in landing from the steamer, and walking about for an hour, we should probably see the worst part of Halifax, as that section near the steamer landing is most wretched and unseemly; and as the people of

Boston would not wish to have their city judged by a person who should wander about an hour in some of the lower localities, so we should not judge Halifax by what we saw of it. There is said to be refined and cultivated society here, and back on the hill-sides the residences of many wealthy and aristocratic families.

I have only time to send much love to dear mother and little Charlie boy, and wish you all much prosperity. Father is calling for this note to enclose in his letter, as the steamer is about to start. Good by. WALTER.

HALIFAX, April 9, 1858.

The incidents of the voyage, after leaving Halifax, may as well be given in a few extracts from Walter's journal, which became quite bulky before the docks of Liverpool came in view.

STEAMSHIP NIAGARA, April 12, 1858.

After a ramble of an hour or two in Halifax, we again embarked. The morning was fine, the wind fair, the ocean clear, and with paddles working, wheels turning, and all sails set, we went crashing, like a city afloat, towards the Old World. I had by this time so overcome sea-sickness as to eat a little, cultivate acquaintance with my fellow-voyagers, joke somewhat mournfully with some poor creatures not as fortunate as myself, and have as good a time as a sea voyage will allow.

Thus Friday and Saturday passed away, and Sabbath dawned upon the deep. O, how different from Sabbath on the land! The waves gliding underneath, the heavy tramp of multitudes on the deck overhead, the wide expanse of waters stretching out in all directions, the moaning of the deep, and the stagnant atmosphere of the ship, all make Sabbath here a strange day.

Others call it sublimely grand. But to me it is no Sabbath. I want the holy hush of a quiet home; the church bell sounding out from city and village; the sudden outpouring of the people, filling the lately deserted streets; the sacred front of the house of God; the swell of the organ; the anthem of the choir; and the sacred stillness of the sanctuary. The Catholic wants his crucifix, the Churchman wants his prayer book, the Dissenter wants the associations of plain, simple, Puritan worship; but on shipboard there is so much noise and confusion that I cannot make it appear like the calm, still, quiet, holy day.

At the proper hour we all assembled in the

dining saloon for religious services. There were several ministers on board, and after the ship surgeon had read the beautiful English Church service, one of them preached a discourse from the words of our Saviour, " And I, if I be lifted up, will draw all men unto me." The sufferings and death of Christ were described, and the Saviour presented as the hope of the world. There were present at that service Jews and infidels, Catholics and Protestants, and all joined in singing the sweet songs of praise to a common Lord. The laws of the ship's company require the English service to be read on Sunday, and until recently the delivery of sermons by any other than an Episcopal clergyman was strictly prohibited; but a few years ago a stir was made about it, and the agitation has brought about a change, and now Protestant ministers are invited to preach, whatever may be their sentiments.

April 13.

To-day I went down into the regions occupied by the mammoth engine — a huge mechanical Behemoth. It seems like descending into Hades; the blazing fire crackling and roaring, the intense heat, the coal-black firemen, who seldom come up into sunlight, the ponderous machinery, and the continual rumbling, hissing, steaming, give an idea of the world of bad spirits as described by poets and orators, and make you feel as if you had come into the vestibule of Dante's Inferno; and though no Virgil comes to conduct us through, yet present fancy can do what absent Virgil does not.

About sixty tons of coal are consumed daily, or seven hundred and twenty tons in a voyage of a dozen days. One hundred and ten men, including officers, cooks, stewards, porters, and sailors, are required to get this immense floating hotel across the deep.

With father, I have been looking at the cooking department, and to me it was a matter of surprise how, in such a little cook room, food could be provided for two or three hundred persons with so much regularity and precision.

Much of our time on board is spent in eating — breakfast at eight o'clock, lunch at twelve, dinner at four, tea at seven, and a late supper between nine and ten, if any wish for it. Father says that all these meals are furnished with a punctuality and promptness that would do credit to the Revere House or St. Nicholas. I think I might imagine I was dining at some great hotel, did not every lurch of the ship make me think of sea monsters and shipwrecks.

April 14.

The steamer is ploughing the ocean in noble style, and we shall soon see the coast of Ireland. The chief feature of our voyage thus far has been a view of several icebergs. The first was seen on Saturday evening. It was a huge lump of ice of chalky whiteness, and lay like a mammoth rock on the bosom of the deep. It was estimated by competent persons to be about one hundred feet long and sixty feet high. It looked cold and cheerless, and had the weather been thick and foggy, would have been a very unpleasant and dangerous neighbor. Father tells me that the great danger in crossing the Atlantic comes from two causes — fire and ice. The former, on board the royal mail steamers, is provided against. The discipline of the crew, the skill of the commander, the means for extinguishing the flames, and the substantial and safe manner in which the vessels are built, form sufficient insurance against fire.

But there are scarcely any provisions to be made against ice, scarcely any thing to do but to maintain ceaseless vigilance. Should one of these steamships strike an iceberg, with her speed of twelve miles an hour, she would probably be destroyed at once. I was told to-day by an officer of this ship that the ill-fated Pacific was doubtless lost by collision with ice. The iron steamer Persia, which started from New York about the same time, ran into an iceberg, which fortunately had been softened by the action of sea and sun. So great was the speed, and so firm her iron sides, that she drove into the floating mass of snow and ice nearly half her length, carrying away her wheel houses, and doing serious mischief. There she was wedged in with the ice. A critical examination took place ere any attempt was made to move her, and fortunately she was found to be firm, and after some trials was relieved from her perilous position.

The poor Pacific probably met some huge, hard iceberg, and, running on fearful speed, came in collision with it, and was sunk at once, not a single man returning to tell the awful tale. It is terrible — in a foggy day or night the iceberg cannot be seen one hundred feet ahead, and as speed is scarcely ever slackened, the danger is fearful when the monsters are near.

On Sunday morning, also, we saw a huge iceberg, supposed to be about one hundred and seventy feet high, and seven hundred feet long. It had three lofty pinnacles, and wore the same dead, chalky appearance as the one seen the previous evening. On the afternoon of the Sabbath, the cry went through the ship, "An iceberg, an iceberg!" and we all rushed on deck to see one directly in our path. It was indeed a most magnificent spectacle. Its proximity to us caused the mercury to fall in the glass several degrees, and the whole sky assumed a dismal appearance. The sight of this one sea monster was worth all the toils and perils of our ocean voyage thus far, and more than compensated for all our sufferings. At first it looked like a huge cliff of chalk. As it came nearer, its position changed, and it looked like an immense headless dromedary. Then it assumed the appearance of a cluster of round towers, thickly set together; and as we sailed within half a mile of it, and had a full, fair view, it took the shape of a dismantled castle. We could seem to see the huge Gothic windows, the high pinnacles, the wide doors, the lofty proportions and icy amplitude of an elegant structure.

I asked Mr. Tenant some questions about the icebergs, and from him derived much valuable information. Floating down from the north, and drifting into warmer water, they are often undermined, and at times roll over with a mighty crash, making the very ocean boil with fury. A large part of the ice is below the sur face of the water, and I can easily conceive the danger of collision with such a monster. The fine view obtained of this "sea-demon," as I heard father style it, I think I shall never forget; its outlines are now as vivid in my mind as when I was gazing upon it. We, however, soon left it in the distance — the mighty thing which, perhaps, had been forming for hundreds of years in the cold north seas, now destined to dissolve and glide beneath the keel of the noble ship, and mingle with the waters of all climes.

On Saturday evening the passengers were greeted with the cry, "Land, land!" and soon the deck was crowded. Some, who had not been out of their state rooms for days, were anxious to obtain the first glimpse of the coast of Ireland. Among the rest, Walter and Minnie were straining their eyes to see, they knew not what. Walter at length discerned what was said to be land, a long, low, narrow, cloudy-looking line, which at first seemed to be hardly distinguishable from the clouds about it.

"What land is that, father?" asked Walter.

"It is Tory Island, on the coast of Ireland. We are going in the north passage."

"What is the north passage?"

Mr Percy explained. "You know, my son,"

he said, "that Ireland lies directly in the way of a vessel from Boston bound to Liverpool, and in order to get into St. George's Channel, which separates England and Wales from Ireland, a vessel must go up around the north, or down around the south coast of Ireland. We are going in through the north passage. Sometimes the south passage is taken."

"What are the advantages of the north channel?"

"It saves fifty or sixty miles in the distance."

"Then why is it not always taken?"

"Because in the winter season it is more dangerous; and the British steamers in the winter generally take the south passage."

"When shall we arrive, father?" asked Minnie.

"I cannot tell, but probably some time to-morrow."

"O, dear me! I wish we could get there to-night. We have been cooped up in this steamer so long that I want to go on shore."

"Be patient, my child; we shall get there in good season."

On Sabbath morning, the coast of Scotland was in view, and land was not lost sight of again. The Isle of Man was passed in the fore-

STEAMER NIAGARA.

noon, and the Niagara entered the River Mersey about noon. The pilot came on board, and Captain Wickman, who, during all the voyage, seemed to be pressed with the great weight of his responsibility, at once became sportive and familiar and seemed a new man. The great burden of care was removed from him, for he knew that if any accident befell the steamer now, the blame would not be his. When the houses of Birkenhead came in view, and the captain's house could be seen in the distance, he went out upon the wheel house, and waved his white pocket handkerchief — a signal answered by the beating of some heart that waited for him there.

All was now confusion below and eager expectation on deck. Below, the porters were getting out the trunks, and preparing for the Custom House officers, who were expected on board. As soon as the ship came to anchor, a steamer came out and took away the mail bags, and some of the officers of the Niagara. Minnie, as she saw the tug about to put off, said to her father, whom she found calmly conversing with Mr. Tenant, "Come, father, come and put our baggage on board, and let us get ashore at once."

Walter laughed; he was posted.

"Not so fast, my child," said Mr. Percy; "our baggage must be examined first."

"Examined? What?"

Again Walter laughed, and this time Mr. Percy joined, and a pout was seen on Minnie's lips.

"Sis, I'll tell you," said Walter. "When certain goods are brought into this country, as father tells me, they are subject to duties."

"Duties! what are duties?"

"Why, taxes, which go to support the government. And our baggage will all be searched, so that the Custom House officers may be sure we have nothing which is subject to duty."

The matter was more fully explained to Minnie by her father, and soon she had a practical illustration, for the officers came aboard, and thrust their hands down into trunks, overhauling the cigars of the men, and the fancy boxes of the ladies, causing those who had the former to think smoking a costly luxury, and those who owned the other to think Custom House officials very inquisitive men, prying into ladies bandboxes and bundles very unceremoniously.

But the whole was soon over, and the passengers, with their baggage, were taken into a tug, and carried up to the wharf. Here the children were almost bewildered with what they saw and heard. A multitude of cabmen, policemen, porters, and spectators crowded around them, and for a time it seemed difficult for them to retain their footing. But Mr. Percy called a driver, who brought a carriage, and the whole company, including Mr. Tenant, were driven to the Waterloo Hotel; where, after tea, seated in a comfortable room in this tolerable hotel, Walter made the following record in his journal: —

April 18.

Here we are, at length, in Liverpool, the greatest commercial city of the world, as I have read. We reached the city at four o'clock on Sunday afternoon, and went at once to the Waterloo House, where we soon found ourselves quietly entertained. As I landed, I felt as the old crusader did when he reached Palestine, and saw the towers of the city of Jerusalem shining in the sun — prostrated himself on the ground, and kissed the earth. I was almost willing to imitate the example of the old hero, when I first set foot on this soil, after days of sickness and weariness. I was very willing to exchange " life on the ocean wave " for life on the solid land; where knives and forks would not dance together on the table, and where our bed at night would not, now and then, take a notion to stand on the headboard or footboard, thus reversing the position of the sleeper to a most uncomfortable degree, — but where his head and feet would always be in their proper places, no longer at the mercy of the storm, the winds, and the waves.

Thus our voyage is ended. We have had the usual events and excitements; we have seen icebergs, steamers, vessels of all descriptions, and have escaped any serious storms. The acquaintances formed are about being broken up, and we now wander each his own way. Some press on at once to the great city — London; some, like ourselves, propose making the tour of Ireland first, and others are scattering in other directions. Our plans are all made for a grand tour of the continent of Europe.

Chapter III.

GLIMPSES OF LIVERPOOL.

On Monday morning, Walter and Minnie were awake betimes, and ere Mr. Percy had fairly opened his eyes, Walter stood by his bed, with the question, " What shall I do for a journal? My paper is exhausted."

" I'll tell you, Walter," said Mr. Percy, after fully waking up — " I'll tell you what to do. In all these European cities there is for sale letter paper with views upon it. I think you will find, on letter paper, of the size you want, many views of Liverpool. You can get these views, and use the paper for your journal, and when we get back to Boston, if you keep the sheets clean and write neatly, I will have them bound up for you, and they will make a capital book."

" What a notion, father."

" Yet a good one ! "

" Who ever did so ? "

" No matter who ever did so. If the plan is a good one, be the first to adopt it."

" I will."

"Our minister, who was in Europe a few years ago, I remember, made a journal in this way, which was very interesting to all who saw it. The paper on which these plates are printed is generally good, and the views illustrate what is written, and fix in the memory the places seen."

"Yes, sir, I see the plan is a good one, and I will adopt it. There is a bookstore near by, and if you will give me a quarter of a dollar, I will run out and get some, and be back before you are up."

"A quarter of a *dollar?*"

"O, I forgot; we are in Liverpool, and I must have a *shilling.*"

The money was furnished, and Walter and Minnie went out to make the purchase. At the bookstore the views were found, and the selection made, and before Mr. Percy appeared in the breakfast room Walter had returned and written nearly half a page.

"Father, don't you think it most time for the breakfast bell to ring?" whispered Minnie.

"They do not ring any bell."

"Why not?"

"Walter some time will tell you that they do not have one long table and a definite hour for dinner, at English hotels, but whoever wishes dinner or tea gives the necessary order, and it is brought."

"Have you ordered breakfast, father?"

"No, not yet, but Walter may go and do so."

"Me, sir?" queried Walter.

"Yes, my son; you might as well learn now to do these things; so go and see what you can do about it."

Walter went to the servant, who stood waiting for orders, and said, "I wish to order breakfast."

"For how many?"

"For three."

"What will you have?"

"O, I don't know."

"How can I bring it then?"

"Let me see; I'll think."

The servant smiled, and Mr. Percy looked on, but thought best not to help his son out of the dilemma; and indeed he did not need to, for Walter spoke out promptly, "We will have coffee, eggs, and mutton chop."

The servant hurried away, and soon the table was covered with food, of which all partook with excellent appetites. While they were eating, Mr. Tenant joined them, and proposed some plans for the day. "We must do our work in Liverpool very hastily, as we must leave in a short time," he said.

"Well, where shall we go first?" asked Mr. Percy.

"I think we had better see the docks first, as they are the peculiar attraction of this city."

It was so agreed, and breakfast being concluded, a cab was engaged, and the whole company set out to see the docks. These docks are artificial basins built of huge blocks of stone, and the water in them is so enclosed as to float the vessels all the time, whatever may be the depth of the water in the river outside. They are built between the Mersey and the town, guarded from storms, and filled at high tide. Many of them can be entirely drained at low tide, or kept full, as circumstances may require. These docks, built at an immense expense, are capable of protecting a vast number of vessels, and distinguish Liverpool from all other places. As you approach the town, the shipping seems to be in the centre of the thickly-settled place. High walls and toppling warehouses can only be seen, with masts, flags, and pendants rising or moving above them and beyond them. Each dock has its water gate, and when any vessel wishes to go forth, the tide being up, the gate is opened, and she is turned out.

The extent and magnificence of these docks,

which are all surrounded with warehouses and stores for the reception or sale of goods, will be seen when it is stated that the Salthouse Docks occupy an area of nearly five acres, and cost three million dollars; the Albert Dock covers an area of nearly eight acres, and cost about four million dollars; the King's Dock has an area of more than seven acres, and cost nearly four million dollars; the Queen's Dock covers an area of more than ten acres; the Coburg Dock covers about five acres; the Brunswick Dock covers nearly thirteen acres; and several others nearly as extensive.

All these docks were visited by the party, and they failed not to mark with admiration the facilities for shipping purposes, and with pleasure the fact that in these vast basins were vessels from almost every clime. Walter and Minnie were much amused at what they saw, especially with the sailors who were hurrying round, and using odd expressions, and with the crowds who were constantly landing at the piers. The Mersey was full of vessels, some coming in and some going out; some with white sails all spread, and some with paddles, funnels, and steampipes in full blast. The scene was exciting, and as the party stood gazing on, Walter recalled a few lines which he remembered to have read some time before, and which he thought must have been written with this view in the poet's eye: —

> "A thousand keels the subject wave divide,
> Float with the flow, or stem the ebbing tide —
> Winged messengers that haste, with sails unfurled,
> To barter produce with some distant world.
> With oar and paddle, sail and thundering steam,
> They row, they cleave, they plough the Mersey's stream —
> That stream which, fretted by a thousand prows,
> No silent rest, no liquid slumber, knows;
> Whate'er the hour, whatever winds prevail,
> Behold the outward and the homeward sail!"

"Well done, Walter; your memory is good, and no description of the scene now before us could be finer," said Mr. Tenant.

Leaving the docks, the party rode to the Sailor's Home — a large, elegant building devoted to seamen. This "Home" is the means of saving hundreds of poor sailors every year from destruction. It is a gem of architectural taste and beauty, and is always filled with the sons of the ocean. Walter and Minnie went into the reading room, and conversed with the hardy sailors there, one of whom took the young people through the building, into the neat, tidy sleeping rooms, into the spacious dining hall, and even into the kitchen. As they went from room to room, Walter's usually clear eye began to flash with unwonted fire; and when he returned to his father, he said, "O, how I wish we had such a grand 'Home' for the sailors as this in Boston."

"We have 'Homes,' my son."

"Yes, sir, but they are not like this."

"And still, humble as they are, they may be accomplishing as much good."

"Ah, Walter, you would make a good curate for Father Taylor," said Mr. Tenant, laughingly.

"I should like to be," said the lad, his whole face lighting up with noble enthusiasm.

Leaving the "Home," the party rode away, and in passing the doors of one of the old churches, saw that some service was being held within. The driver reined his horses up at the door, and a large sign on the edifice informed the stranger that marriages were celebrated at that hour on that day of the week.

"We *must* go in, father," cried Minnie. "O, the fun of going to a wedding this morning!"

"If we *must*, we must, Minnie," replied Mr. Percy; "but I think it will be a loss of time."

They all entered the church, and witnessed a novel spectacle, which "did pay," as Minnie afterwards declared. Eight couples or pairs were standing at the altar, strangers to each other, but all being married in one service. The clergyman hurried through the service, jumbling up his words, and making the whole thing ludicrous. As soon as the service was over, the minister hurried to an anteroom, and the sexton took the couples in one by one to sign the record and pay the fees; and as Walter passed by the door, he saw the happy bridegrooms making the change, and counting out the shillings, just as regularly as if they had, instead of marrying a wife, been buying a pound of tea or a loaf of bread.

"Father, father," cried Minnie, "I hope none of these men will make any mistake when they come out of that little room, and take the wrong bride."

"Hush, hush, my child."

"It would not matter much," whispered Walter in the ear of his sister; but a grave look on the face of Mr. Percy hushed their merriment.

Leaving the church, they again entered the carriage, and when seated Mr. Percy said to Minnie, "What o'clock is it by your watch? Is it not about time to dine?"

Minnie took out her watch, and, in vexation, exclaimed, "This watch, which you gave me for a birthday present, is not good for any thing at all."

"Not good for any thing! Why, it cost sixty dollars."

"Well, you may see. Here it is about noon, and my watch says that it is only seven o'clock. What do you make of that?"

"Perhaps Walter can tell us. Is it the fault of the watch or Minnie herself, my son?"

"O, it is Minnie that is out of time."

"What do you mean?"

"Why," said Mr. Percy, in explanation, "the time differs. Your watch would be just right if you were in New York or Boston, but the London time is about five hours ahead of New York time. It is now five minutes after seven by your watch, which was set before you left home, and, knowing the difference in the time, I am sure it is just twelve o'clock here. I am as confident as if I held my watch in my hand, and that, you know, I set this morning by the clock at the hotel."

"But I would like to know more about it."

"Walter will explain the whole to you some time, as I fully explained it to him on the voyage."

"I have a calculation and a drawing which I made while on shipboard, which Minnie can have to look at. It shows the time, relatively, in different places, and the mate of the steamer told me it was right. It shows the time in five different places," said Walter.

Minnie was much pleased with the drawing, which is found on another page, and expressed the earnest wish that Walter would explain how it is that time differs so much in different places.

By this time the carriage had reached the hotel, and the whole company were soon enjoying themselves in different ways, while dinner was being prepared for them. Minnie had thrown herself upon the bed; Walter was filling up his journal; Mr. Percy was writing a letter to his wife; while, we regret to say, that Mr. Tenant had his feet on the sill of the open window, and was making his mouth a smoke pipe for the fumes of a cigar, to the use of which he was somewhat devoted.

"I think," said the latter, holding his cigar between his fingers, "that one would hardly select Liverpool as a place of residence, independent of business considerations. The streets are irregular, and filled with seamen and dock laborers of the lowest class; houses, stores, and workshops are strangely mixed together; and ignorance and poverty are distinctly seen."

"And yet," replied Mr. Percy, who had finished his letter, and was folding it, "we have seen some fine public buildings, among which are the Exchange, the Sailors' Home, St. George's Hall, and several others; and I am told that there are parks and cemeteries of great beauty."

"True; but you see that the city is devoted to commerce, and only those men live here who —— "

"Dinner ready, sir," cried a servant, opening and shutting the door; and our friends repaired to the table, where a fine piece of English roast beef was set before them, which, with sharpened appetites, they discussed with great hilarity. At the table the question was asked, "Well, where shall we go this afternoon, Walter?"

Walter had been looking over the guide books, in search of objects of interest, and replied, "I should like to go to St. James's Cemetery, said to be a lovely spot."

"I have no objection to that," said Mr. Percy.

"Nor I," added Mr. Tenant.

But Minnie voted in the minority. "O, do not go there. Walter is always looking after cemeteries, tombs, and old buildings. Let us go to the Zoölogical Gardens, for I should much rather see leopards, lions, and monkeys, than tombstones."

"We can go to both places, my child, so that both of you can be gratified."

The carriage was called, and away they rode to St. James's Cemetery, situated in a deep dell surrounded by high hills, in which excavations are made for tombs. Almost the first object which meets the eye, on entering, is a Grecian oratory, in which are several monuments to the crumbling memory of the dead. On every side are statues and effigies, the poor memorials of once living, moving men. This burial place is one of much rural beauty, and, from its picturesque situation in what was once a stone quarry, in the sides of which are several sculptured galleries of catacombs, draws the attention, and claims a visit from every stranger. The great object of interest, however, is the marble statue of the Right Hon. William Huskisson, formerly one of the most distinguished citizens of Liverpool. The statue stands in a circular oratory, and was made in Rome by an English artist.

It did not take our party long to go through these grounds, and glance at the various objects of interest, as the whole area contains but about forty-four thousand square yards, and, as a minute inspection of such a place was not needed, the visit to this home of the dead was soon concluded. In returning, the whole party called on the minister, who lives in a handsome stone house near by, who gave them several items of useful information in relation to the grounds. During his conversation, he called the oratory a "Greek Hypæthral temple," a term which Minnie could not understand, and which she resolved to ask Walter to explain, but which she forgot to do, as her mind was not on oratories and temples, but on the elephants and lions she expected soon to see.

They next drove to the Zoölogical Gardens, where the remainder of the afternoon was spent. They went from the cage of one animal to another, from one cage of birds to another, until they had seen the whole — elephant, lion, monkey, and all. One or two amusing things occurred here. There was a huge ostrich closely confined, and when Minnie laid her hand on the bars of his prison, he snapped at her, and she was obliged to withdraw her hand. But as the bird stood with his head against the bars, she took out her gold pencil, and tapped him on the bill.

"You had better let him alone, little girl," said the keeper.

"O, he won't hurt me;" and she continued tapping his beak with her jewelled pencil. The bird watched his opportunity, and seized the pencil in his mouth, and swallowed it.

"Well, I declare," cried Minnie.

"What is the matter?" asked her father.

"Matter enough. This great ugly bird has swallowed my pencil."

"I told you to be careful," said the keeper.

"That is just the way with Minnie; she is always getting into trouble," said Walter. "That is the third new pencil she has had within three months."

"Well, I didn't know the creature would eat it."

"Well, let it go now," said Mr. Percy; "only be more careful another time, my daughter."

"I think, Minnie, you are growing somewhat extravagant," added Mr. Tenant, "to feed your pet birds on gold pencils, at five dollars each."

"O, what plagues men are!"

Returning from the gardens, our friends sought rest, for they had had a wearisome day. In the evening Walter and Minnie staid in their rooms, and amused themselves as best they could, while the two gentlemen went out to find some kind of night entertainment. On turning the corner of a street, they saw a placard on the wall, informing the public that a mass missionary meeting was to be held that evening at Great George Street Chapel, where the very venerable Dr. Raffles preaches. Expecting to hear some of the celebrated men of Liverpool speak, they directed their steps to the church, which is an elegant structure, the principal elevation of which consists of a semicircular portico of fluted columns, reminding one of the temple of Jupiter Stator, surmounted by a dome, and occupying a most beautiful situation; being, internally and externally, a most imposing edifice. They entered the church, and were fortunate enough to hear two of the most celebrated men of Liverpool. One of them was Dr. Raffles himself. Mr. Percy had long known of this eloquent clergyman, the successor and biographer of the lamented Spencer, who, while bathing in the Mersey, was drowned, one of the brightest lights of the English pulpit being extinguished suddenly. On the present occasion, Dr. Raffles made a speech — a venerable man, with his head whitening, yet speaking with a mighty power; speaking until his own soul glows with his theme; until the perspiration stands in great drops upon his noble brow; until the audience lean forward, as his grand periods roll out; until each man clutches his purse, ready to pour its contents into the plate when it comes; until breathing is almost suppressed, and the whole assembly is melted, or thrilled to the most intense emotion.

He was followed by Hugh Stowell Brown, a man as popular as Dr. Raffles, but of a different style entirely. He made a telling speech, and the interest with which he was watched, and the enthusiasm with which the sentences, as they fell from his lips, were caught up, showed the estimation in which he was held.

The gentlemen were surprised to find that all the telling things were applauded, even in a religious meeting, which at times was as uproarious as a political convocation in our country could be. The speeches were interrupted with constant cries of "Hear, hear;" and the stamping of feet and clapping of hands seemed to Mr. Percy to be quite out of place in the house of God. However, he was very glad to hear these two celebrities of the Liverpool pulpit, the latter of whom has done much good and gained much influence by lecturing to the working men.

On his return from the meeting, he found Walter writing in his journal, and Minnie asleep on the sofa, the latter of whom was soon sent away to bed, and the former read what he had written in his diary to his father for correction; and so ended a laborious day in Liverpool.

There were other objects of interest in the place, which were visited on the following day. And among these is worthy of mention the new

St. George's Hall, a noble public building erected for musical entertainments, and justly an object of pride to the citizens of the place. The floors are marble, set in beautiful, many-colored mosaics; the walls and ceilings are profusely and appropriately ornamented; the decorated pillars and arches create a fine effect, while one of the largest and noblest organs in the world, which cost thirty-five thousand dollars, pours out its rich, liquid music over the people. The children, who had never seen any such hall before, were very much pleased, and Walter rapidly took pencil sketches of the end which contained the organ.

"Is there any hall in our country so splendid as this, father?" asked Minnie.

"No, my child, I think not."

"Why not?"

"Because our plain people think that plainer structures best subserve the public good. The price of evening entertainments in such a hall as this would be so great, that few would attend them, and the property would be unprofitable."

"Shall we see many halls like this?"

"Not many halls like this; but before you return to Boston, you will see buildings such as you have never imagined."

Having seen this great hall, it was suggested that a jaunt be taken to Birkenhead, which rises from the banks of the Mersey, nearly opposite Liverpool. The suggestion was adopted, and soon in a ferry boat the river had been crossed, and our friends were wandering about in Birkenhead.

"This seems to be a new town," said Walter.

"Yet," replied Mr. Percy, "forty years ago the whole population was less than fifty persons, and now they are numbered by scores of thousands."

As they passed along, they found Birkenhead to resemble less an English than an American city, and it seemed to them to be to Liverpool what Brooklyn is to New York — the sleeping chamber of a metropolis. Many wealthy men who do business in Liverpool reside at Birkenhead, which is more quiet than the giant city on the other bank of the Mersey. It is well laid out, has its parks, and churches, and objects of interest, all of which our party visited. None of them were of more interest than the ruins of an ancient abbey founded in the year 1190 by the Baron of Dunham, Haman Massie, and long occupied by monks, who trod its pavements, and made its walls echo with their songs. Several arches, pillars, and other evidences of the former beauty of the structure which now lies in ruins were seen. An examination of the town occupied most of the day, and the party concluded to dine before returning; and as the eating houses were plenty, they found one where they were well accommodated, and dined at a much cheaper rate than they could have done at the hotel. The dinner over, they all repaired to the ferry, just as the shades of evening began to gather. Walter remarked that the ferry arrangements were the most perfect he had ever seen, and instead of being built as cheaply as possible, as some of ours are, the piers, and tide walls, and gateways seemed to have been constructed with an eye to elegance, rather than to economy, and indulged in some remarks not highly complimentary to American ferries. His father checked him with the remark, that this ferry belongs to the town of Birkenhead, and not to private owners or a corporation, and that all the profits are expended in beautifying the surroundings.

"Yes," added Mr. Tenant, "Walter must remember that our country is young; we have less wealth, and cannot expect the perfection in these things which is attained in England."

Thus conversing, the party crossed the ferry, and walked up to the hotel, where the evening was spent in social intercourse with several American friends who were in town at that time. Some days were occupied in viewing the place and becoming acquainted with its people and institutions, and one bright morning the company started for Ireland, going on the way a little into the interior.

A couple of cabs took the whole party with their luggage to the station house, a magnificent edifice, the front of which, with its thirty-six three-quarter Corinthian columns, and its grand arched doorways, cost thirty-five thousand dollars, which, added to the cost of the rest of the structure, with its glass roof and heavy finish, makes the building a very expensive one.

As here we are to take the cars, it may be well to describe the railroads and rail carriages, which differ from ours. Minnie made herself quite merry over them, when she saw them, but probably had some reason to think afterwards that all the advantage was not on our side. There are three classes of cars, and for either of them the traveller purchases his ticket, as he may choose. Having secured his ticket, he is generally sent into a separate room, where he finds others who are to ride in the same class cars. If he be a third-class passenger, he does not see those who are to ride in the first and second-class cars. They too are shut up, to await the hour of starting. When this arrives, the first-class passengers are taken from the room where they have been held in durance, and seated comfortably in the cars without noise or jostling, and the doors are closed, and, in some instances, locked. Then the second-class passengers are seated, and at length the third. The cars are short, being only about eight or ten feet long and six wide, and are frequently divided by a partition as high as the head of a person sitting; or, if they are longer, are divided into separate apartments. The first class are well arranged, well fitted, and comfortable; but the fare in them is so high, that few besides the nobility and the wealthy ride in them. The second-class cars are destitute of cushions, and almost every other comfort. On the hard seat, with the straight back, the passenger is compelled to sit, with his feet covered up with boxes and baggage, gazing upon the placards which are pasted up on the sides and ends of the car. Generally these cars have two seats, each holding five persons — one half looking into the faces and trampling upon the feet of the other half. The window, or ventilator, as it should be called, is a small, square aperture in the door, like the window of a coach, and generally has a slide of glass, but sometimes only of wood, to keep out the rain In these cars we do not have the comforts that we find in our own cars. There is no opportunity to walk about, and scarcely any to stand up, some of the cars not being high enough for a tall man. The third-class cars are somewhat longer, and have rough seats, like some of our baggage cars, and are no more comfortable or convenient. The fare is higher for this class than in our country for the best, and more ride in this than in either of the other classes. The distances are generally short, and people sacrifice ease to economy.

The railroad arrangements are all much safer than among us. The roads are better built, the tracks are better laid, and there is a confidence which one never feels when in the express trains on the American side of the Atlantic.

But to return to our friends whom we left in the station house. Seating themselves in the cars, the train started out through a dark, smutty tunnel, which is a most wonderful artificial excavation beneath the town. This tunnel is six thousand six hundred and ninety feet long, seventy-five feet wide, and fifty-one feet high, and passes directly under the place, while over it rise churches, houses, halls, and places of trade and industry. He who had never rode in a rail car would hardly be willing to begin by riding through this subterranean passage. The oppressive darkness, which can be *felt;* the cold, a damp chill, which pierces to the bones; the glaring lamp on the engine, and the screaming of the iron horse, — all render the five minutes spent under the streets and temples of the great mart of commerce most unpleasant and disagreeable.

As they went on, Minnie clung to her father, who felt a trembling of her body, as the cars rolled swiftly into increasing darkness, and she hardly dared to breathe, so fearful was the passage through; and not until they emerged, and began to dash along in open sunlight, did she breathe freely.

The party arrived at the old town of Chester, after a circuitous ride of some hours, and a stop at one or two places on the way. Chester is but a half hour's ride from Liverpool; but our friends preferred to take one or two interesting towns in the course, and it was high noon when they found themselves on the way to an inn in this ancient place.

"Stop," said Walter, when some distance from the station house.

"What for, my son?" asked his father.

"I have left my new gutta percha cane in the cars."

"How careless!" said Minnie.

"Wait, and I will run back," said the lad.

He had purchased a new gutta percha walking stick, finely mounted with silver, just before starting, and had left it in the car; and when he reached the station house the train was gone, and he did not find the article, or gain any information as to what had become of it.

"Never mind, Walter," said his father; "I will buy you a new one. But you must be more careful in future."

Walter inwardly resolved that that should be the last thing he would lose if carefulness could do any good; and on the party went.

WALTER'S TIME TABLE.

(See page 82.)

Chapter IV.

A WALK ON CHESTER WALLS.

An antique looking inn, of the old style and time, standing in one of the proudest streets of Chester, had a look so inviting that our travellers entered and dined there. In an old wainscoted room, with dim and venerable pictures on the walls, the table was set, and without much effort of imagination Walter put himself back a hundred or two years, into the old times when every innkeeper was a portly man, rotund and merry, or a bonnie woman, with a pretty daughter; and every inn had some fancy name, varying from Black Bear to Green Dragon, from White Swan to Black Eagle. The hostess was an English lady of forty years, who doubtless could say,—

> "I am an innkeeper, and know my goods,
> And study them,"—

and who seemed as much at home in her business as Giles Gosling or old Harry Baillie could be. A hundred years ago the inn was a public institution. Men's characters and fortunes were made and lost there; it was the cradle and the tomb of revolutions; it controlled alike the parson and the hangman; a sort of third estate, of which the keeper was the autocrat. And the "Swan Inn" reminded our travellers of the old times; and Walter, who had revelled in English history, grew enthusiastic in praise of "mine host," as he termed the woman who answered his calls. The swan painted on the old swing sign, the old sideboard just as it used to be, the long bench for the people waiting to be served, all helped the illusion.

"This old room looks as if it might have sliding panels and secret doors," said Walter.

"It is more likely to have rat holes and mice nests," suggested Minnie.

"Try the panels, Walter," added Mr. Tenant.

Walter tried the panels, rapped them with his knuckles, which, though they gave back a hollow sound, did not move, and Minnie only laughed at him for his pains.

Just then dinner was brought in. It consisted of fried ham and eggs, with nice white bread and coffee. The ham was cut in such thin, delicate slices, the eggs looked so fresh and nice, the bread was so white, the cream so rich, the butter so sweet, and the coffee so clear, that all thoughts of sliding panels and secret doors gave place to intense satisfaction with the excellent entertainment provided by the hostess; and Walter ate as voraciously and unpoetically as if he had not been trying to indulge in romance over an old, dilapidated inn, and an old, wretched room therein.

Dinner over, the party went out to see the town; and a quaint old town they found it to be. It gives the traveller a very fine idea of the style of the middle ages; for enough yet remains of the old English fashion, that one seems taken back two or three centuries. The place retains all the peculiar plainness of the English architecture of a dead and buried age, and the times of William the Conqueror seem here to be handed down to us. As they walked along, looking up at the curiously constructed houses, Walter asked his father, "Who founded this place?"

"I don't know, indeed. Sir Thomas Elyot, in 1520, declared that Magus, son of Japhet, was its founder."

"What, almost as old as the flood?"

"That would make it so; but Ranulph Higden, a monkish historian of the place, tells us the founder was a giant, Leon Gawr, who began by building mostly under ground."

"And which statement can we take?"

"Probably neither is correct — but every thing around us indicates that the city is very ancient; and probably. if you say it is one of the oldest in the world, you will not come far out of the way."

"When do we have reliable information in relation to its condition?"

"About the times of Roman power in the island we begin to get positive information, and after that it figures conspicuously on the pages of history."

By this time the party had arrived at the flight of steps over which they were to reach the top of the old Roman wall that entirely surrounds the town. The ancient Britons had mud walls where these now stand; but when the Romans in their ruthless power rolled over the land, they were swept away, and the massive towers and thick battlements we now see rose in their place.

There is not a city in England where the walls are so perfect as these. They form a rampart around the town, and furnish one of the most delightful promenades imaginable. The visitor can look down upon the crooked streets, quaint houses, and ruined churches on one side, and out upon the wide, open country on the other side. These walls are a little more than one and three fourth miles long, and every foot is rich with historic interest. Britons, Saxons, and Danes have shed their blood upon them; and they stand to-day, after many centuries have beat upon them, monuments of human passion and the fates of war. No stranger ever goes into Chester without taking a walk upon these walls, and no traveller who has once walked around will ever forget the strange impressions made upon his mind.

Commencing the circuit, under the guidance of an old man, who was born in Chester, and who told Walter he had never been ten miles away from the town, they were pointed to the place where once stood the "Saddler's Tower," which, falling into a dangerous state of decay, was taken down nearly a hundred years ago. It was once the meeting place of a company of saddlers, and derived its name from this circumstance. A few paces on, and a majestic tower rose before them. The old man said, "This is called the Phœnix Tower. Hundreds of years ago, it was known as Newton Tower."

"Why is it called Phœnix Tower now?" asked Walter.

"Because," said the guide, "the figure of a phœnix is over the front of it. Do you see it there?"

"Yes, and I see an inscription. What is it?" Walter read aloud,—

KING CHARLES
STOOD ON THIS TOWER
SEPTEMBER XXIV. MDCXLV. AND SAW
HIS ARMY DEFEATED
ON ROWTON MOOR.

The guide then gave a long description of the battle. Charles had suffered several terrible defeats; his army had been driven from point to point, and now he stood gazing upon the battle which was to test his strength, and, perhaps, decide the fate of his kingdom. He waited not long; the contest became more terrible, and soon the shouts of the soldiers of Cromwell announced to him that his cause was lost, and that he must flee. Soon his soldiers came crowding in upon him, followed by the psalm-singing legions of the Protector.

This was the account given by the guide, and Walter said he would remember the statement, and compare it with the facts, and see if it was correct; which he afterwards did, and found the old gentleman was not wholly right in his description, as the guides are not always expected to be.

From the top of this tower a fine view was

obtained, and the gentlemen stood admiring it; but Minnie and Walter plied the old gentleman with questions about the battle. They were absorbed in that, and the guide, seeing their earnestness, told them he would answer any questions they might ask about it.

"What did the king do," said Minnie, "when he saw the men run?"

"He walked slowly and sadly down over the steps by which you came in, leaning on the arm of an honorable citizen of the place."

"How long did he stay here?"

"He escaped the next day, and went to another part of the kingdom."

"What became of him?"

"He was executed — beheaded within three years afterwards."

"And what did the opposing army do when the king had gone?"

"They staid in front of the city until famine and starvation compelled the governor to surrender; then the gate was opened, the soldiers marched in, destroyed the fortress, defaced the public works, and did much mischief."

Leaving the tower, they came to the north gate, and the children, on looking over the wall, saw that a street passed under it, and that over the street was a noble arched gate, amid the stones of which the humble ivy clung — a gateway which, in years past, had admitted kings and conquerors to the ancient city. It was curious to look down upon the queer houses below, with their peculiar roofs and sides, looking as if they belonged to a dead age.

Next they reached the watch tower, called Morgan's Mount, on which, in times of war, a battery is placed; and woe to the enemy that comes within reach of its guns. Walter was anxious to know whence the tower derived its name, but the guide could not tell him. While the rest went on, he ran up the winding staircase, to an open space on the top, and had another fine view of the country, at which he gazed with so much interest, that he almost forgot that he was alone, and was called to his senses by the shout of his father, who wished to hurry him along. He found the rest of the party in front of the Goblin Tower, a semicircular structure, now called Pemberton's Parlor.

"What is this?" said Walter, as he came up to his friends.

"The Goblin Tower," answered the old guide.

"Why do they call it so?"

The old man then related a long ghost story,

A WALK ON CHESTER WALLS. 85

from which he said the tower derived its name. But as such foolish stories never should be told, we will not repeat what he said. It is foolish for any one to believe in ghost stories, and little boys have far more reason to be afraid of wicked men, and even of their own wicked hearts, than of ghosts and goblins.

Next the attention of the party was attracted by some modern baths, which were reached by a flight of stone steps. The day was warm, and Minnie was weary, and so it was agreed that the company should sit a while on the wall, resting and enjoying the prospect, while Walter indulged in the luxury of a bath, which was obtained for a penny, or two cents. When he returned they started on, and soon came to two towers, near each other, one called Bonewaldes-thorne's Tower, and the other the Water Tower. Walter tried to pronounce the name of the first, but made poor work of it, and Minnie asked him if he was talking Dutch or Hindoo. Both of these towers are much shattered. The Puritan cannon was planted on Bruera's Hill, at a little distance, and these riddled towers tell of the mischief done by them. In them are kept many trophies of other days, which Walter and Minnie examined with much care. Here are rusty swords and daggers, with the blood of murder yet eating in; here are trophies taken in battle, mingled with the peaceful evidences of better days.

Thus the party went on, by the infirmary, and the city jail, the remains of Black Friars Monastery, the castle, and many other things which were odd and pleasing to the eye. They made a hasty visit to the armory of the castle, where they saw thirty thousand stands of arms. The children were amazed at this display, and Mr. Percy told them that these arms were kept here in time of peace, but if war should be declared, they would be taken to supply the soldiers who would enlist.

As they again stood on the wall, the guide said, " Here you see the River Dee flowing along by the town."

" Where?" inquired Walter.

" Why, right before you, my little man."

" What, this insignificant stream here?"

" You must remember, my son," said Mr. Percy, " that the rivers of England are not like those in America. Here a stream which in our country would be too small for a name, is dignified with the appellation of 'river,' and is looked upon as an important feature of the country."

" I have read so much about the 'noble Dee,'

that I thought it would be like the Hudson, or, at least, as large as Charles River."

"Well, if you don't like the river, look at that bridge, and see how you like that," said the guide, pointing to a bridge thrown across the stream. "It has but one arch, but that is the largest stone arch in the world."

"How much is the span?" asked Mr. Percy.

"Two hundred feet," was the reply.

"What do you call it?"

"Grosvenor's Bridge, and it cost thirty thousand pounds."

Soon they reached a flight of steps, leading down from the wall, and the attention of the children was directed to them. "There," said the guide, "are the Wishing Steps."

"Wishing Steps!" said Walter; "what are they called so for?"

"I will tell you, as it was told me long ago. If any person will wish for any thing, though it be a crown or a throne, a kingdom or a fortune, and run up these steps once, and down again, and then up to the top the second time, *without taking breath*, he will have his wish."

Walter went to the foot of the steps, and thought over what most he wished, and then started up the steps; but when he arrived at the top the first time, he found himself out of breath, and, with considerable vehemence, declared the steps "a cheat, for nobody could go over them twice without taking breath."

As they went on, laughing at Walter for his pains, they came to the place where they first mounted the wall, and, passing down the long flight of steps, found themselves in the street below. Minnie was amused at the names of the streets. She found them so curious that she wrote some of them down on a paper — such as Watergate Street, Common Hall Street, Linen Hall Street. And then there were many lanes, such as Love Lane, Fleshmongers Lane, (so called because many butchers formerly resided there,) the Old Law Lane, and many others. And then there were *rows*, — such as Paradise Row, Brokenshin Row, Pepper Alley Row. There are "places" running in from the street, and one of these Minnie noticed was called "Puppet Show Entry." All these curious names are derived from something in the past, which now has no existence; but the names remain, as curious as the city itself.

The houses of Chester should be described. Many of them were built centuries ago, and have all the characteristics of the olden times. They are erected so as to protect the sidewalk in front, the second story projecting over the street, and supported on pillars, so that a man may walk the whole length of a street in a rainy day, looking into the windows of the shops, and not be wet. These rude arcades furnish shelter from the storm, and protect from the burning rays of the summer sun.

In many of these houses the frames are seen, being on the outside, and filled in with plaster or cement. A house thus finished makes a grotesque and lively appearance, the plaster being drab or white, and the beams, posts, braces, and other timbers, being painted red or green. Some of the modern houses are built in this style to conform to the old ones, which are falling to pieces with age. It is not seldom that the fronts of these houses are profusely ornamented. There is an old structure known as Bishop Lloyd's House, which is very old, its history running back many hundreds of years. The whole front is covered with carvings of Scripture scenes, and though ancient and unique, it stands as a wonderful specimen of art; and the party lingered long before it, gazing on it with admiration.

In passing from spot to spot, they came to the Stanley House, so called because a family of that name built it for a city palace. On its front are carved the figures 1591, indicating the date of its erection. It has three elaborately carved gables, and is probably one of the oldest timber houses in the world; and many go to look at it with interest and pleasure.

They came to the "YATCH INN," and as Walter looked upon its venerable walls, he asked his father what there was about the inn that made it seem familiar.

"I don't know, my son."

"Well, I have heard of this inn somewhere, and there is some history connected with it which I cannot now recall."

Mr. Tenant assisted the memory of Walter, and asked him if he had not heard of the anecdote of Dean Swift, the witty, eccentric, and sacrilegious ecclesiastic, which is found in the hand-books of Chester.

"No, I never did. What is it?"

"Why, it is said that the dean came to Chester, and stopped at the 'Yatch Inn,' and from his rooms sent out for a number of clergymen to come and dine with him. They did not know the dean, or, not caring to make his friendship, did not come. The table was spread, and groaned beneath the luxuries placed upon it, but the dean was the only person to sit down to it. He was chagrined and shamed by the treatment, and scratched upon the window

GOD'S PROVIDENCE HOUSE.

of his room the following couplet, which remained for a long time:—

> 'Rotten without and mouldering within,
> This place and its clergy are both near akin.'"

There was another house in Chester that interested the whole party very much; and even Minnie, who said she hated old buildings and fallen churches, could not but view it with emotion. In Watergate Street stands the old timber house on the front of which is a very striking inscription —

GOD'S PROVIDENCE IS MINE INHERITANCE.

The house is called "God's Providence House," and the children were very anxious to know its history. The old guide told them the story, which affected them very much. He told them that in the year 1652, a disease called the "Sweating Plague" was prevalent in England, and Chester was dreadfully scourged by it. It appeared mostly among men, but few women being smitten by it. In that dreadful year, about one thousand persons died in this little place of this malignant disease. The city had been ravaged by war, but this new besieger seemed invincible, and the noblest citizens were hurried into eternity. Silence reigned in the streets, and the grass grew where, until now, the dust was pressed by the tramp of man and beast. One house, that now before us, was unvisited by the King of Terrors. It was occupied by a Quaker family, and was the only one in the whole place where death had not set his fatal signet. This one family alone escaped the pestilence that walked in darkness and wasted at noonday. The house now bears the inscription above mentioned, and is an affecting illustration of that providence that wrote " passover " on the doorposts of this one single habitation, when all others in that city were scourged with death.

They found an old lady sitting in the doorway, plying her needle, and Mr. Percy addressed her thus : " Do you have many visitors to see this house ? "

" Yes, scores every day."

" Then you make it profitable."

" O, no ; they do not come in, but content themselves with gazing on the outside."

" Do you know who had the inscription carved on the front of your house ? "

" The good man who lived here when the plague prevailed. He did not do as many others do when spared by Heaven's bounty and beneficence."

"Ah, what is that?"

"Forget in a day God's providence."

"Good woman, you are quite a preacher."

"No; God's providence preaches from the inscription on this house; but there are few that profit by the preaching."

Mr. Percy put a shilling into Walter's hand, who gave it to the woman, who smiled her thanks, and the party passed on until they came to "the cathedral," which occupies a spot on which the Romans once built a temple to Apollo, and where, still later, had stood an object of veneration — a Druid temple. An abbey, in which devout monks chanted and sang, took the place of these, and in 1492 this gorgeous, majestic cathedral rose in massive grandeur and elegant proportions. It is built of red sand, stone, and time has been rounding its edges, until they look now like huge, red, round paving stones, set in the wall. The niches, which abound on the outside of the building, are now tenantless, the images and effigies that once filled them having fallen out; and the time-worn aspect of the whole makes an impression on the beholder which he does not soon forget.

Within, the huge dimensions, the Tudor arches, the beautiful stained glass windows, monuments to the memory of the illustrious dead, — to Dean Swift, John Moore Napier, and many others, — the massive stone screen of the choir, the stairs of heavy oak, the various chapels, and all the adornments of a cathedral, are grand and impressive as one can imagine. The nave is one hundred and sixty feet long, seventy-four and a half feet wide, and seventy-eight feet high; and standing in such a place, one can easily transport himself back to other days, can call up the olden times when abbots ruled and monks sang beneath this immense roof. The furniture of this cathedral is very rich and elegant. The pulpit is of stone, wondrously carved; the Episcopal throne is composed of relics from the Abbey of St. Werburgh, the pious daughter of Queen Ermenilde, and which are said by the Papal authorities to have performed astonishing miracles; and all the various objects of interest are very attractive to the stranger.

Walter had never seen a cathedral before, and his admiration was unbounded. He stood looking upon the huge arches, or walked through the transept, or gazed into the cloisters with solemn awe, while Minnie was nervous and impatient to be gone.

"Come, Walter," said his father; "we must go."

"O, I could stay here a whole day. I never saw any thing so grand as this rich tracery and these beautiful canopies. I would like to stay and study out the intricate designs on these windows, and decipher the characters on the tombs."

"But we have not time for that; unless we go now, we shall be obliged to leave some other interesting place unvisited."

As they passed out, Mr. Percy dropped into the hands of the old sexton a piece of money, that being the fee expected of those for whom he opened the doors. They then repaired to St. John's Church, in a most superb location, and very ancient in its appearance. It was founded by Ethelred in 689, in response to a vision which he had, in which God told him to build a church on the spot where, in the first hunt, he should take a white hind. He was not disobedient to what he considered a heavenly communication, and this spot was selected as the result, and the church erected, and consecrated to St. John the Baptist. In 1057 the edifice was repaired, and strengthened, and made more beautiful. In 1468 the steeple, a huge tower, fell down of its own weight, coming through the building to the earth. It was rebuilt, and again in 1572 it came crashing down, and was reërected on the west end of the nave, and stands there to this day, one hundred and fifty feet high. The hands that reared this noble pile were long ago palsied in death, and moulded to dust, but their work endures. The main part of the church still stands, but in so dilapidated a condition that the bells in the tower are seldom, if ever, rung, lest the jar should bring the whole structure down in one promiscuous ruin. The stones which compose the edifice have been rounded at the edges by time, like those in the cathedral, so that they will hardly hold together. And yet wonderful art is seen in this old edifice and the adjoining ruins; lofty arches, noble pillars, well-turned windows, letting in the "dim religious light," and the steeple towering towards the skies, impress the mind of the beholder with veneration and awe.

On the west side of the tower is a niche, in which stands a statue of Ethelred, petting the "white hind" which he saw in his vision. When the tower fell, this statue was uninjured, and now is an object of much interest.

"Do you suppose that God came to Ethelred in a dream, father?" asked Minnie.

"No, my child; he might have had such a dream, but God does not now communicate with men in that way."

"And do not the people, by keeping this statue here, show that they believe the story?"

"No; for the inhabitants of Chester are very intelligent, and they only wish to perpetuate what they believe to be a mere fancy of the king."

The party left the church, it being near time for the cars to start. They walked to the station house, which is a very fine edifice, where Walter found the cloaks and umbrellas of the party, which he had left at the "Left Baggage Office." Connected with this station, and with almost all on the English railroads, there is a deposit office, where articles may be left until called for. On payment of a penny or two, the article is taken, and a check given for it, and the office is responsible for any loss. This is a great convenience for the stranger who wishes to stop in a town a few hours, but does not wish to go to a hotel.

In the "Refreshment Room" of this depot, Walter found a long table covered with writing materials — pens, ink, and paper; and having purchased some views of Chester on letter sheets, he sat down to record the events of the day, and we will open the book and read what he says.

CHESTER, April, 1858.

A visit to Chester is worth a voyage across the ocean; and the day I spent there will long be remembered. The old wall, and the churches, God's Providence House, and the funny old streets, have been daguerrotyped upon my memory; and if this was the only place we had to visit, it would be worth the voyage. I do not like to leave the place; its memories crowd upon me, and call after me, and I would like to stay long amid these old scenes, the glory of which is in some degree gone.

> "But many a relic still is left
> To shadow forth the past."

"Cars coming, Walter," interrupted the writing, and soon the whole party were settled back in one of those luxurious, first-class English cars, where a man can sleep at night almost as well as he can on his quiet bed at home. The door was locked, the train began to move, the old towers of Chester faded away, and soon the mountains of North Wales appeared in view.

Chapter V.

RIDE THROUGH NORTH WALES.

"WE have just crossed the line into Wales," said Mr. Tenant, as the train rolled on.

"How large is Wales, Mr. Tenant?" asked Walter.

"About as large as New Jersey."

"How do the Welsh people differ from the English?"

"In several respects. The language differs, the habits and customs of the people differ, and one would hardly suppose he was so near the great heart of England, while journeying in Wales. The Welsh are the descendants of the ancient Britons, and their language has Celtic peculiarities."

"The oldest son of Queen Victoria is called the Prince of Wales. I have often wondered why — can you tell me?"

"O, yes, I can; and the story is a short one. In 1276, Edward I. became involved in a war with Llewellyn, Prince of Wales, and finally, having conquered the Welsh people, annexed the territory to his crown, and made his oldest son Prince of Wales. This son was born in Caernarvon Castle, and afterwards became King of England. And ever since then, the oldest son of the English sovereign has held the title of 'Prince of Wales,' and the distinction is little more than nominal."

"Suppose the sovereign of England has no son — what then?"

"The oldest daughter is created Princess of Wales."

"I have heard that Wales was a hilly country."

"Very hilly, as you will see as we go on. It has some very high mountains, among which is Mount Snowdon, which is three thousand five hundred and seventy-one feet high."

"Is not Wales well supplied with old castles?"

"It has some, and we shall see a few of them as we go on, if the night does not set in."

Thus conversing, they rode on through a very fine and picturesque country, by many very pleasant looking towns, and within sight of many old castles. Walter made acquaintance with an old gentleman who had come into the car, and of him he gained much reliable information as they progressed. "Did you ever hear of Christmas Evans?" asked Walter.

"O, yes, my lad."

"Did you ever hear him preach?"

"Many a time."

"Was he as eloquent as the few extracts of his discourses which I have seen would indicate?"

"He was a very eloquent man, and lived about ten miles from the place where we now are, and his memory is much cherished by the Welsh people, among whom he lived and labored."

Minnie called the attention of Walter to the fact that the farther they went, the poorer the people seemed to be. The cottages along the way had very poor walls, and simple thatched roofs, and in the fields women by scores were at work.

The party arrived at Menai Straits just as the dark mantles of night were falling on the earth. These straits separate Wales from the Island of Anglesea, and are spanned by two bridges of much note. The Suspension Bridge was the first of the kind built in Europe; six years were required for its construction, and its total cost was about one million dollars.

"How does this Suspension Bridge compare with that over Niagara River, below the Falls?" asked Walter of his father.

"That cost only four hundred thousand dollars."

"Did the same architect design them both?"

"No, the Niagara Bridge was designed and constructed by Mr. Roebling, an American, and this by Mr. Telford."

Over the Menai Straits is also thrown the famous Britannia Tubular Bridge, one of the wonders of the world; and the cars dashed into its hollow passage, and emerging on the other side, stopped to give the passengers time to go back and see it.

"What is the Tubular Bridge, father?" asked Minnie.

"It is an iron tube, stretched across the straits, for the cars to go through."

"An iron bridge?"

"Yes, it is constructed of plates of iron, about half an inch thick, and two or three feet square."

"How are they put together?"

"They are heavily and closely riveted together, making a square tube, wide enough for two tracks, on which two trains can meet, and high enough for the smoke pipe of the locomotive. Strong iron knees and braces add to the strength of the structure."

"Does not the bridge sag some?"

"No, when the most heavy-laden freight train rolls over it, it is not even seen to vibrate."

"How long is the bridge?"

BRITANNIA BRIDGE.

"I do not know the whole length of the bridge, but the tube is about three hundred feet, and is about one hundred feet above the water, and rests on two substantial piers."

"How did they manage to get it up into its place?"

"By some hydraulic process, I believe."

They had now reached the bridge, and found it to be indeed a most remarkable structure — an iron tube, of plates riveted in three thicknesses to appear as one, yet to have the strength of three, resting on its piers as firmly as if the span was but a dozen yards.

"And where are we now?" asked Walter.

"We are on the Island of Anglesea."

"Is that island a part of Wales?"

"It forms one county of Wales."

"How large is it?"

"I think it is about twenty-four miles long, and seventeen broad, and has a population of about thirty-seven thousand souls."

"And how wide is this strait?"

"About half a mile, I should judge."

Having seen the tube, and finding the night so dark that little else could be distinguished, they entered the cars, where the conversation about bridges was resumed.

"I remember seeing it stated," remarked

Mr. Tenant, "that over the River Rhone, near Avignon, in South France, the seat of the popes when they were banished from Rome, and where their old palace, used for a prison, still stands, there is the Bridge of the 'Holy Spirit,'— the somewhat inappropriate and singular title of one of the longest stone bridges in the world, — built six hundred years ago, the first bridge ever thrown across the Rhone. It has twenty-six arches, and is the noblest structure of its kind in France. It was built by a religious society called "The Brethren of the Bridge," and their object was the protection of travellers from the banditti, who, acting as ferrymen, robbed their victims, and threw them into the river."

"Do you know," asked Walter, "which the oldest bridge in England is?"

"That at Croyland, in Lincolnshire, is the oldest."

"When was it built?"

"In the year 860; and none but foot passengers go over it."

"Which is the longest bridge?" asked Minnie.

"The longest in England?"

"Yes, sir,"

"That over the Trent, at Staffordshire, which is built of freestone."

"How long is that?"

"It is fifteen hundred and forty-five feet long, has thirty-four arches, and was built in the twelfth century."

"How long is the famous London Bridge, of which we have heard so much?"

"Only nine hundred and ninety-five feet long.

"You will see," added he, "when you get to London, some of the finest bridges in the world. Those which cross the Thames are very finely built, and you will admire them."

The ride from Chester had been so pleasant, and the time passed away so quickly, that Walter was sorry when he arrived at Holyhead, where the party were to take steamer for Dublin. Though it was late at night, it was resolved to go on, as a steamer would start in an hour or two. They left the cars, and were standing in the station house, when a voice was heard:—

"Supper all ready! hot, hot supper."

It is strange what a voracious appetite is given one by travelling; and though Minnie had taken an ample collation a little while before, she now declared she was "hungry as a bear." And Walter said that there was "not food enough in town for him"— a specimen of extravagant speaking, on the part of each, which sounds very foolish in people, young or old.

The party stumbled through darkness and obstacles into a very comfortable restaurant, where they found all the accommodations for supper, which was relished by all. As they sat at the table, Mr. Percy asked his daughter, —

"What do you think mamma is doing at home, Minnie?"

"Why, she is sound asleep, of course."

"What do you think, Walter?"

"I suppose she is taking tea, and thinking of us."

"Taking tea at this time of night! That would be funny!" cried Minnie. "She is asleep, for it is nearly midnight."

"Do you not remember what we talked about the other day, when you thought your watch was not a good one?" asked Mr. Percy.

"O, yes, yes, I forgot; well, let me see; it is just about seven o'clock in Boston."

"Suppose, Minnie, you could send a telegram to your mother," said Mr. Tenant; "what time would she get it?"

"I think, if the ocean telegraph was laid, she would get our message as soon as it started."

"She would get it some hours before it started," said Walter.

"Worse and worse, Walter," replied Minnie; "by and by you will begin to argue that we shall get home before we started to come out."

"I see, sis, that you need light."

"All I get from you is darkness on this subject. Do sit down some time and explain, for when I meet some one who does not know so much as I do, I wish to appear wise, as my learned brother does," was the sarcastic reply.

Walter would have replied, but his father checked him with a kind word, which changed the subject of conversation, and the supper ended without any more sharp shooting between the young people.

Mr. Percy and Mr. Tenant went out to see if they could form any idea of the place they were in, but came back to the children without knowing whether the town was large or small, for the night was dark, and a drizzly rain and dense fog had set in, and no discoveries could be made.

Chapter VI.

CROSSING THE CHANNEL.

"STEAMER ready! all aboard!" called our friends from the shelter of the friendly restaurant; and they were soon on board a miserable steamboat, used for conveying freight and cattle across the Channel. The regular steamer had gone some hours before the arrival of the late train. A glance was sufficient to assure Mr. Percy that the comforts of that night were few, and that the crossing would be tedious.

The whole party stood a few moments on deck, debating as to the best plans for securing a night's rest; and as the ponderous wheels began to move, they went below. Here they were informed that no berths were provided, but the settees could be used for sleeping purposes. Mr. Percy at once collected two or three cushions, and made a comfortable bed for Minnie, who, wrapping her travelling dress close about her, lay down to sleep. A place was next found for Walter, who had his carpet bag for a pillow, and his father's heavy coat as a coverlet.

Two or three men were already stowed away in the cabin, and Mr. Tenant took a settee, one end of which was already occupied, and Mr. Percy found a comfortable sofa, on which he cast himself. But they were destined to have but little sleep. One of the passengers was an old English officer, who, after our friends were well settled, went into the particulars of a story which he was relating when broken in upon by Mr. Percy and his party. The story related to the wonderful escapes and the dreadful dangers of his military life. The fountain from which he drew his facts seemed to be exhaustless; one thing led into another, and his tale of military wonders, which would have astonished Napoleon or Wellington, seemed interminable. He had been in the Crimea, and was present when General McMahon planted the French flag on the very summit of the Malakhoff, while the dying and the dead lay in heaps all around. At one time he was wounded on the field, and left for dead; at another time he was surrounded with foes, and, with the valor of desperation, cut his way through, and escaped; at another time he led a line of soldiers against overwhelming numbers, and came off victorious. The more the old man talked, the more enthusiastic he became, until the patience of Mr. Tenant was exhausted.

"Look here, my friend," he cried, at length; "did they sleep any in the Crimea?"

"O, yes, we slept, but had sentinels out."

"Well, if you talked as much there as now, I do not see how any body got any sleep."

"I profess to be a gentleman, and know when to speak and when to stop."

"I should judge you to be a volcano of words; and if you have any mercy upon us poor fellows, who have been travelling all day, do stop, and let us get some sleep."

And then he added, "I do not mean to be rude, sir, but really we would like to go to sleep."

The old man drew his head down into his shaggy coat, and said no more; and soon the whole company gave evidence of being in profound slumber. Walter found it to be a tedious, restless night. His hard couch did not do much to rest his weary limbs, and he awoke again and again from a disturbed and unrefreshing sleep, with troublous and exciting dreams. At one time he dreamed that he was at home, and his father was away in Europe, and news came of his death, wringing with sorrow the heart of his mother. Again he dreamed he was on the ocean, and the vessel came in collision with a dreadful iceberg, and was dashed to pieces, and through a long, dark night, and a cold and dreary day, he floated on a huge lump of ice, that crumbled with every wave that dashed against it.

At length the whole company were startled with a terrible shriek from one of the sleepers, who, oppressed with nightmare, raised a terrific yell, that brought every man to his feet. The attitude of the company was somewhat ludicrous. A dim light shone in the cabin, and half a dozen persons, some with their coats thrown off, others with handkerchiefs bound around their heads, stood looking at each other, and saying, "What is it?"

"Father, father, is the steamer sinking?" cried Minnie.

"That is too bad!" was the exclamation of Mr. Tenant.

"Haw, haw, haw," laughed the old soldier.

"Come, friend Tenant, no more sleep," said Mr. Percy.

All this time the unconscious cause of this commotion was lying on the bench, breathing hard, but unmindful of the scene before him. Walter, when he found there was no trouble, lay down again, and tried to sleep, but found the thing impossible; and soon after, seeing his father go out of the cabin, he followed him on deck. The morning was just appearing in the east; several large vessels were in sight, the royal mail steamer was just then going by, and in the distance the long, dark coast of hazy Ireland could be seen. The morning was very fine; the Channel, which is usually rough and boisterous, was placid and smooth; and the view around was charmingly beautiful. Soon Kingston was in view, a town named in honor of George IV., formerly called Dunleary. It has a most excellent harbor, designed to afford a refuge for vessels in distress, and is a few miles from the city of Dublin. It occupies a very fine position, and around it are several interesting ruins. The old castle of Monktown, shattered by the assaults of time and war, is near at hand. The remains of Castle Bullock are close to the pier, and are visited by every one who lands at Kingston. The three castles of Dalkey, erected long ago for the defence of the coast, are situated at a little distance away, and the traveller from another land will find no want of objects of interest even on this rocky promontory of the Irish coast. A railroad is stretched from Kingston to Dublin, and the whole distance is lined with pretty villas, thatched cottages, and the various indications of Irish life.

Slowly sweeping by Kingston, the steamer rode into Dublin Bay, a beautiful sheet of water, into which the world-famed Liffey pours its tumbling waves. The emotions of Walter were peculiar as he saw the monuments, steeples, and towers of Dublin in view. He had seen the Irish people as they exist in America, and had judged very wrongly of the Irish nation by these specimens, and was hardly prepared to see the capital of Ireland rising out of the waves, and crowning the shore as beautifully and gayly as his own Boston rises out of the Atlantic, and crowns the bay of Massachusetts.

"O, how beautiful!" was his delighted exclamation, as he stood on the steamer's deck, and the successive scenes of interest passed before him: and as the morning sun shone upon the city of O'Connell and the great men of whom he had read, he fairly clapped his hands for joy.

"O father," he cried, "I shall like Ireland; I know I shall."

"What makes you think so, my son?"

"Why, the hills look so green, and the sun looks so bright, and the morning seems to dawn so beautifully, that I know I shall like it."

"I suppose you will like it, because you will see old castles and ruins," said Minnie. "I thought so when I heard father telling you of those old castles out there on the headland — Monkey, Bullock, and Duckey castles I believe he called them. As for me, I shall keep my likes until I get to Paris or Brussels."

"Every one to his taste," said Walter, his face kindling with new enthusiasm, as the steamer came near the city, and the public buildings became more distinct.

Soon the vessel touched the pier, and the whole company, with their carpet bags and baggage, leaped on shore, and stood on the soil of Dublin.

Chapter VII.

THE IRISH CAPITAL.

"WELL, they have 'dumped' us down in Dublin, as the natives would say," said Mr. Tenant.

"Certainly they have; and where shall we go now?"

"Have you any hotel on your memorandum, Walter?" asked Mr. Percy.

"Yes, sir, I have the name of the *Imperial*, that some one has given me as an excellent house."

Several men, who had been standing about, now appeared, and their purposes were evident at once.

"Have a cab, sir?" asked one.

"Do you wish for a hotel?" asked another.

"Shall I carry your bags?" inquired a third.

"This way, this way; I will show you to the best hotel," cried a fourth.

"Stop, friends, stop; which hotel is the best one?" asked Mr. Percy.

"The Bilton," cried one.

"The Imperial," cried another.

"Reynolds," shouted a third.

"Prince of Wales," cried a fourth.

And one clutched the baggage, crying, "I drive to Bilton's;" and another laid hold of the children, saying, "Get in, get in; I drive to Gresham." Walter laughed; Minnie was afraid; Mr. Tenant, with a smile, said, "Friend Percy, make up your mind, and decide quickly." Mr. Percy, breaking from the crowd which by this time had gathered around, called a modest-looking young man, who stood with his cab at a little distance, and said to him, "Drive us to the Imperial."

The hungry crowd at once fell back, and the young man, who had lost nothing by his modesty, gathered up the baggage, and assisting his passengers into his vehicle, cracked his whip, and they drove rapidly up into the city. Turning into the beautiful Sackville Street, and passing several fine edifices, the carriage drew up before the door of a comfortable-looking, quiet hotel. At once several porters ran out, and seized the baggage, and led the travellers in.

They were seated in a comfortable parlor for a few minutes, when Mr. Percy was called to select his apartments. He found a suit of high-posted, lofty rooms, all of them somewhat gloomy, but very clean and airy, and at once engaged them at a very moderate sum.

Breakfast was ordered, and while it was being prepared, the party attended to toilet duties, and in arranging their apartments, so as to make themselves comfortable during their stay. As the time they were to remain in Dublin was quite limited, every moment was to be improved; and no sooner was breakfast finished than the day's work commenced. The landlord, at the request of Mr. Percy, sent for a janting car, in which they were to ride through the city.

With this janting car the children were much pleased. It was a vehicle altogether unlike any they had ever seen. It was a two-wheel carriage, something like an old-fashioned baker's cart, with seats on each side for two persons, and one in front for the driver. These seats are back to back, and the persons occupying them sit with their side to the driver, looking outward. Constructed in a light, easy style, it becomes at once a very useful, convenient, and graceful carriage to ride in. One can mount and dismount with perfect ease, and our travellers were charmed with it. In all the places in Ireland visited by them, they found it used by all classes, the high and low, rich and poor.

Gay ladies and noblemen were seen dashing about from place to place, dresses fluttering in the breeze, and the light, fantastic vehicles rolling over the ground with the greatest velocity.

Walter wondered why such carriages were not used in the suburbs of Boston; he thought they would be admirable on the macadamized roads in the vicinity of the metropolis for short pleasure tours.

The hotel from which they started was on Sackville Street. This street is one of the most beautiful thoroughfares in the world, and the Dublin people think no other city can present its equal. Long, straight, and wide, it has many beautiful edifices, and is always thronged by the business men of the place. Several of the finest hotels, the General Post Office, and a number of noted public buildings rear their huge fronts on this street.

About midway between Rutland Square and the River Liffey, in this street, stands the Nelson Pillar, a fine Doric column one hundred and thirty feet high, surmounted by a life-looking statue of that naval hero. There stands Nelson, in his dead eloquence, looking down upon the thousands of people who surge along below, reminding the beholder of one of the

THE IRISH CAPITAL. 123

bravest men, and one of the most revered of all the naval heroes of Great Britain.

The top of this pillar is reached by a winding staircase, which is ascended in the dark, the poor traveller striking his head against the stony sides of the pillar at almost every step.

The view of the city from this monument is very fine, the streets, houses, and public buildings, not crowded and confused, like those of London, but regular and orderly, lying like a map before the eye. The old cathedral, Christ's church, the towering monument to Wellington, the custom house, from the dome of which Queen Victoria looks down in her state dress, are all full in view. The winding course of the Liffey, spanned by its fine bridges, can be traced for miles. The people on the pavements below look like pygmies dwindling away, and the whole view of the city, stretching out in all directions, is admirable.

In the janting car, the party rode out of Sackville Street to explore the city. The people looked after them, as they were easily recognized as strangers. On they drove to the Bank of Ireland, a very noble structure, which faces College Green. In the days of Ireland's glory, ere the power of England had taken away Irish nationality, the buildings now used by the Bank were the Houses of Parliament. The old hall of the Commons is now the magnificent banking room; and instead of Irish orators and statesmen discussing the duties and perils of the nation, bankers and merchants, tradesmen and artisans, meet here to negotiate loans and transact business of a monetary character.

The House of Lords remains much the same as when the peers left it. The ancient chairs, the long table, and the various fixtures of such a room, are all here, as in the days of Irish power, and the room is used only once or twice a year, at the meetings of the bank directors. Where once the throne stood now stands a statue of an English king, and the power which of old held empire here is dead, and the eloquence which once thrilled the souls of listening multitudes has departed forever.

The building covers an area of two and a half acres, and is one of the finest banking houses in the world, far more imposing in its external aspects than the Bank of England. The centre of the edifice in front consists of a grand colonnade, formed of lofty Ionic columns, which rest on noble steps, forming a noble entrance to the building. Over the high doorways are statues of Hibernia, attended by her handmaids Fidelity and Commerce. The whole edifice is a monument of art worthy of any city. The lofty Ionic columns, the massive walls, the gorgeous porticoes, the statues, and emblematic designs, add to the perfectness of the whole, and give a richness and nobility to the structure which to be appreciated must be seen.

By the kindness of an official connected with the bank, the party were allowed to go through the building, inspect the private rooms, look into the vaults, and become familiar with the mode of transacting business, which to Walter was quite a novelty.

The next visit was to the celebrated Trinity College, founded by Queen Elizabeth nearly three hundred years ago, on the site of an old monastery. As they drove up, Walter asked if the buildings about to be inspected would equal the buildings of old Harvard.

"We will see," said Mr. Percy, who had some idea of the college, and knew its high rank.

They found the buildings to consist of three quadrangles, and covering an area of some twenty or thirty acres. The front, facing College Green, is three hundred and eight feet long, elaborately finished in the highest style of Corinthian taste. A servant conducted the party into the theatre, or exhibition room, hung with portraits of noble personages, and embellished with monuments to the illustrious dead; into the chapel, a noble building, itself a magnificent church; into the library, which is a building two hundred and seventy feet long, having several apartments, and over one hundred thousand volumes; into the manuscript room, where are large collections of valuable manuscripts; into the refectory, where is a dining hall larger than many churches, the walls hung with portraits of Ireland's noblest men; into the provost's house, a miniature palace, and into many other buildings belonging to the cluster.

In the main square there is an elegant bell tower ninety-two feet high, which presents to the eye a grand appearance. Walter inquired of the porter how many students were connected with the college, and was told that the number at that time was about seventeen hundred. He gave a low whistle, expressive of his surprise, and as they went out of the gate, leaving the porter's face all covered with smiles, Mr. Percy having put into his hands a crown, the lad turned to his father, and said, —

"All this in Ireland!"

"Yes, Walter, and much more, as you will see when we drive about the city, which will make you go away with better ideas of Ireland than you ever had before."

Minnie was pleased with the students whom she saw. "What nice young men they are, father!" she said; "see how they touch their caps to us as they pass."

One of the young men, passing at the moment, and catching the merry twinkle of her eye, turned somewhat abruptly, and said, "You like the college; do you?"

"O, very much."

"And would you like a little sketch of it to carry home to your friends in America?"

"O, very much indeed; but how did you know we were Americans?"

"Because your *accent* told me so; and the gentlemen, who, I see, are going on without you, look like Americans. Here is the sketch which I have just taken; it will be a pleasure for me to give it you."

"You are very kind; thank you, thank you very much; but please tell me who I shall say gave it?"

"That is another thing, my child; but you may call me student O'Donnell," and laughing, bade her "good by."

Minnie ran on looking at her picture, which was a very well taken sketch of the college, the green, and the bank in one view, with the noble equestrian statue of William III. in the foreground.

Another place visited by the party was the Castle, near the centre of the city. This pile of buildings disappointed Walter very much. He had heard of Dublin Castle, and had pictured to his mind a rough tower, on a ledge of rocks, bristling with cannon and waving with flags. But he found only a cluster of buildings in the heart of the city, now occupied as the town residences of the lord lieutenant and the officers of state, and seeming to be a general metropolitan police station. His father, however, gave him some historical facts in relation to the Castle which interested him very much, told him that it was founded by King John in 1206, and described the various scenes of which it had been the centre, in the troublous times which Ireland has seen since then.

The party also went to the Cathedral of St. Patrick. There are two cathedrals in Dublin, and one of them stands on the site of a church once occupied by the patron saint of Ireland himself, and is a very fine old edifice, three hundred feet long, surmounted by a noble tower and spire two hundred and twenty-one feet high. This old cathedral made a decided impression on the mind of Walter. It seemed as if he would never tire of gazing on the grand ceilings, the well-turned arches, the beautiful arcades formed by them, and the stalls for the ecclesiastical dignitaries on days of worship.

"What are these banners for?" asked Minnie of her father, on observing a large number of flags hung in the nave and choir.

"These," said her father, "are the banners of the dead and living knights of the order of St. Patrick, a very illustrious organization which exists in Ireland."

A few questions brought out all Mr. Percy knew of the knights of St. Patrick, and Walter concluded he had obtained a thread which would take him back into the mysteries of the past. Several fine monuments and memorial slabs are found in this cathedral.

"Here," said Mr. Percy, "is the monument of Dean Swift."

"I have often read of Dean Swift," said Walter; "who was he?"

"He was an ecclesiastic, who was born in the county of Tipperary about the year 1667. He was a noted wit, a man of eminent abilities, but entirely unfit for the clerical office. His first name was Jonathan."

"I thought it was Dean."

"No, 'Dean' was his religious, or ecclesiastical title. He was dean of this cathedral. He wished very much to have an English bishopric, and Queen Anne was about to give him one, but some unfortunate articles written by him, one known as the 'Tale of a Tub,' a piece of humor indecorous and unbecoming a divine, were urged against him, and he never secured the coveted honor. He was bitter in his attacks upon other writers, among whom was his relative, the excellent Dryden, against whom he aimed some of the most pointed of his satires. But here is the tablet of Hester Johnson."

"Who was she?"

"If you will read the writings of Dean Swift, when you return to America, you will find references to 'Stella.' She was a lady of great excellence, who was privately united in marriage to the dean, but the marriage was never publicly recognized. She died of a broken heart."

While they were looking at these and other monuments, reading the inscriptions on them, a strain of beautiful music fell on their ears — a strain of music swelling louder, and deeper, and heavier, filling the whole cathedral with the rich, mellow, varied sounds. All turned to where the noble organ stood, from which the unseen player was producing such exquisite melody.

"This organ," said a bystander to them, "is

one of the purest, sweetest-toned instruments in the whole kingdom."

They listened a while, and then took a look down into St. Patrick's well, a deep, dark well under the church. From this well, it is said, St. Patrick drew the water which he applied to the first Irish convert; and, as such, is regarded with veneration by the people, and interest by all strangers. As the party left the church, the fine chime of eight bells in the tower, were playing an old familiar tune, which reminded them of " Home, sweet Home."

They next rode to Christ's Church Cathedral, a plain edifice, of less interest than the other. The church is hung with banners, ornamented, or disfigured, as one's own taste may decide, with monuments of the dead; on the gallery are carved the arms of all the viceroys of Ireland, and all about are evidences of the olden times, when were blended with religion, the strifes of politics, and the clamors of war. The church is in sad decay, and broken buttresses, and disfigured walls, meet the eye in every direction.

" And now, children, what else have you for us to see?" asked Mr. Percy, as they drove away from the cathedral.

" To the barracks," said Walter.

"What are the barracks?" asked Minnie.

"They are the houses where the soldiers live, sis. Do you want to see them?"

"O, yes, any thing is better than these churches that are all ready to tumble down on our heads. Heigh-ho for the red coats!"

They were soon at the barracks of the infantry, and, after some little trouble, were allowed to enter the square. Here they found the regiment practising some drill exercises, in full uniform. The evolutions were so finely gone through, the music was so exhilarating, the red coats of the soldiers, and the shining arms, made so brilliant a display, that the whole party felt richly repaid for coming to the place. They waited until the drill was finished, and the men dismissed to their quarters, and then went into the barracks.

"Are these real soldiers?" asked Minnie of Walter.

"Certainly."

"Have they ever been in war?"

"I suppose some of them have. They may have been at the Crimea."

"They look finer than our 'play-training-soldiers' in Boston, who never saw a battle; don't they?"

"Yes, sis, these are stout and hearty men,

who doubtless are ready to go into battle at any time. Our citizen soldiers train for amusement, and are not called on except in case of riot."

"I remember, Walter, that the companies in Boston were called out when that slave, poor Burns, was carried away."

They went into some of the rooms where the men sleep, into the rooms where they mess, and saw the general style of life the soldiers live; and, as they turned away, Walter said, "I should not like to be a soldier."

"Certainly," replied his father, "this mode of life must be very disgusting; full of temptations to dissipation, and having little about it to exalt, ennoble, or dignify."

"Do these men have much pay?" asked Minnie.

"No, my child, not as much per diem as a boy in America would have for wheeling in a ton of coal. These soldiers have a mere pittance — a few pence."

They now turned towards the hotel, as the shades of evening were gathering, and they had worked hard all day. The evening was spent in animated, cheerful conversation, in which the children took an active part. At some times Mr. Percy would not have allowed them to be so forward in the utterance of their opinions; but now, as his object in travelling was, in part, to benefit them, they were encouraged to talk freely, and express themselves fully in relation to all they saw.

"I do not find here the wretchedness that I expected," said Walter.

"You have formed your opinion of the Irish in Ireland from what you see of the Irish in America, forgetting that the better class of Irish people do not leave home."

"But I have read such dreadful accounts of famine and want, that I expected to see Dublin filled with paupers, and to ride through streets in which misery would stare out upon us from the windows of all the houses."

"Those accounts are often exaggerated, or they may apply to one particular locality, or they may be true of one season. Doubtless Ireland has vastly improved within a few years, but I think your impressions of the country never were strictly correct."

"I think as hard things have been said about our own country," added Mr. Tenant.

"It can't be, Mr. Tenant," replied Walter.

"Well, Walter, I can prove what I say. I have in my pocket an old paper which I found among my baggage to-day, from which I wish to read an account."

"We will listen with all our ears," said Minnie.

Mr. Tenant took out his paper, and read in a full, clear, manly tone, as follows: —

"Last week a single soup house gave out a ton of corn meal, two thousand loaves of bread, and fourteen thousand pints of wholesome soup, thus supplying daily twenty-five hundred persons with food. Within gunshot of this soup house are more than twenty cellars in which the destitute victims of the grog-shop seek refuge every night at a penny a head. All colors and both sexes turn in promiscuously at nightfall, lie down in bunks that rise one above the other against the bare walls, and there spend the night in utter darkness, the soft side of a pine board being their only bed. For two cents extra they may have some filthy straw to lie on. Each one pays his penny as he enters, and none are admitted without it. In the confined atmosphere of these vile dungeons the victims of the dram-shop doze the night away. How these unhappy creatures escape suffocation may be left for science to determine. But when morning breaks, though it be cold and crisp, with snow a foot deep upon the pavement, the keepers of these dens throw open the door, and warn the miserable congregation that it is time to get up and clear out. Sick and shivering they rise, and hungry and unrefreshed they are driven forth into the street, there to wander off to the friendly soup house, or otherwise to pick up, by theft or beggary, subsistence for another day, whose close will be a repetition of the scenes of the preceding one."

" What part of Ireland was that ? " asked Minnie.

" Where could that be ? " asked Walter ; " certainly not here."

" Can you not guess where it was ? "

" In Cork ? " said Walter.

" In London ? " said Minnie.

" No, it was not in Cork, nor in Dublin, nor in London, nor in ⎯⎯ "

" Where was it ? " asked the children in one breath.

" It was in the beautiful city of Philadelphia."

" Impossible, Mr. Tenant, impossible," exclaimed Walter ; " why didn't we get it in American papers if it was true ? "

" That is the way foreign papers talk about our country," said Minnie.

" No, I did not read from a foreign journal. You must not lay the blame on an exaggerating editor in London or Dublin," replied Mr. Tenant.

"Do let me take the paper," said Minnie, all excited.

"Please tell me what paper you read from?" asked Walter.

"The New York Tribune."

"Can it be?"

"Here it is in black and white, from the pen of a Philadelphia correspondent. Now, children, what I wish to say is, that such statements are often made in relation to European countries, and we think there is a horrible state of destitution; we take the single case, and suppose the whole land is like it. That is not reasonable, and if you had read in the Dublin Nation, or the London Standard, a similar account of any locality in this country, you would have thought the condition of the people most pitiable."

Walter acknowledged the justice of Mr. Tenant's reasoning, and retired to rest that night with a different idea of Ireland and the Irish than he had ever had before. Indeed, Mr. Tenant himself found the city of Dublin to be a much cleaner and more tidy and quiet city than he had anticipated, and felt that the Irishman in the new world might well look back with pride and pleasure to the metropolis of his little sea-girt isle.

The next morning the children were up betimes, and had ordered breakfast long ere the gentlemen were awake; and when they, somewhat late, entered the breakfast room, they found their morning meal smoking hot upon the table. Having despatched that, they called the driver of a janting car, and went forth to see the objects of interest. During the drive, they came to the city residence of the late Daniel O'Connell, a plain, substantial-looking structure in one of the most fashionable streets.

"Who was Daniel O'Connell?" asked Minnie.

"He was an Irish statesman," answered Mr. Percy, "of great eminence, a true lover of his country, and a man whose name is respected, and whose memory is revered, in every land wherever the Irishman wanders."

"Was he a soldier?"

"No, he was a civilian, and led one of the great parties that exist in Ireland, and became the idol of the whole people."

The driver of the car, an enthusiastic admirer of the departed statesman, had become intensely interested in the conversation, and breaking in upon Mr. Percy, exclaimed, —

"And, sure, Ireland will never see his like again."

"Perhaps she will. God always raises up

men for emergencies, and if Ireland wants men to lead her councils or her armies, she will have them."

The Custom House was an object of interest, and Mr. Percy, who was a practical merchant, wished to see if the inside of that edifice was equal to its exterior; so they drove in that direction, and in a few minutes they were in front of this magnificent temple of commerce.

The Custom House stands on the north bank of the Liffey, and is three hundred and seventy-five feet long, and more than two hundred feet deep, and has four highly-ornamented fronts. The river front is finished in Doric order. Huge pillars, bold entablature and cornice, statues of Neptune and Mercury, Industry and Plenty, alto-rilievo emblems, the whole crowned by a noble dome, forms at once an object of decided beauty and imposing majesty. The other fronts are finished in a style of great taste, and the mountain granite, of which they are composed, presents a noble specimen of solid masonry.

The interior is divided into courts, and various offices fill the whole edifice. An immense business is done here, but in a very quiet way, and no little admiration was expressed by Mr. Percy and his companions of the admirable arrangements, and the numerous conveniences for despatching the business of such a house; and the party rode away, uttering many expressions of pleasure.

The next building visited was the "Four Courts," a noble edifice erected for the accommodation of the law and equity courts. It stands on the river, and has a front of four hundred and fifty feet in length, between Whitworth and Richmond Bridges. The exterior of this building is covered with emblematic designs, conceived and executed in the best of taste. The centre of the building has a Corinthian portico, supporting an elaborately carved pediment, above which rises a circular lantern, which is lighted by large windows. On each side of the centre are squares, and in them are the law offices. These law offices and court rooms are very spacious, and present to the mind of the stranger a very favorable idea of the people whose taste and genius require these magnificent arrangements. Walter, who was pleased with every thing he saw, could not help contrasting this edifice with many of the court houses he had visited at home; but some information given him in relation to the working of the courts, the amount of business centred here, while, in our own country, the law business is diffused, being transacted very largely in the shire towns of the various counties, led him to see that, though we have few buildings that, in all respects, compare with this, we have, on the whole, more and better accommodations for those who have the most business to do.

All day was occupied in seeing the fine buildings, parks, and private houses, and the next day was taken up in riding through the city, along the river, over the bridges, and through the outskirts. The plan was, to go through all the best streets first, to see all the aristocratic residences, and the houses of the men of wealth and fashion. This they did hour after hour; and when they had seen enough, Mr. Percy said to the driver, " Now take us through some of the worst and most degraded portions of the city. We have seen the best parts; now we want to go into the places where your poorest people live; drive through such streets."

" I will, sir."

Soon they were rolling along humble, but by no means filthy streets, and Walter asked, " Are these the worst streets ? "

" They are the worst I know of."

The travellers could hardly believe this, for they expected to find something so much worse, that they could not put a dark look upon any. thing, and the ride terminated without seeing any streets more degraded than many found in our own land.

On returning to the hotel, Mr. Percy said to Walter, "My son, the steamer will leave Liverpool at noon to-morrow, and I propose writing to your mother, and, if you like, you may do the same."

Walter eagerly embracing the proposal, at once sat down, and wrote the following note: —

DUBLIN, 1858.

DEAREST MOTHER: —

Across the ocean I greet you, and from this land of strangers and strange things I send home to you, not only these few poor lines, but my whole heart, that yearns for you. One thing, one thing only, I want in my journeying — the presence of my mother. Minnie and I often talk about you, and every night when we kneel down and say our prayers, we breathe your name, and Charlie's too.

I closed my last letter when just arrived at Liverpool. We spent some days in Liverpool, exploring the wonderful docks, and becoming acquainted with the various works of art. Liverpool is a great city, but a very crowded and confused one, and the traveller wishes to get out of it as soon as possible; and we were not sorry when the time came for us to depart.

THE IRISH CAPITAL. 143

Leaving Liverpool, we crossed over to Ireland, stopping, on our way, at the interesting old town of Chester, and glancing, in our rapid passage, at the scenery of Wales, with its old castles and abbeys, and its quaint old towers, and quainter people. I admire Ireland, for the whole country is so beautiful at this season, that it seems a perfect garden, from its deepest valleys to its highest mountain peaks. Why the inhabitants should want to leave such a land we can hardly tell. The large cities of Ireland are very fine. Boston cannot be compared, in some important respects, with Dublin, and other places compare favorably with our best towns. We rode, to-day, through the worst and lowest streets of Dublin, and found none as bad as North Street, in Boston, or the Five Points, in New York; and I shall leave with a better impression of Dublin than I ever had before.

I have talked much with the people, and father says I am getting to be very inquisitive; but I would rather incur the odium of being inquisitive, than to go through Ireland without getting any information.

We find all classes here interested in America and American institutions. We scarcely meet a man who does not have some relative in our country. One has a son at New York, another a cousin in Wisconsin, and a third some friend in Boston. The people, however, are beginning to get the idea that going to America is not altogether what it has been represented to be. Emigrant agents have made the people of this land think that in our country dimes grow on bushes, and dollars are as plenty as potatoes. But so many have come over, and written home discouraging tidings, that others are afraid to venture over.

You would be surprised to know what a traveller I have become. I believe I could go the round of the continent of Europe without any one to look out for me; and I have remembered that you have often wished you could have some one to go with you to Saratoga or Niagara Falls, when father was closely confined by his business. Now I shall learn so much about men and things, see so much of the world, and become so familiar with the way of getting along in it, that I shall be able to escort you about in the summer season, and you will not be obliged to depend on the changes in the money market, or be subject to the ups and downs of business.

We are all enjoying ourselves finely; or "hugely," as Mr. Tenant persists in saying; or "beautifully," as Minnie expresses it. Father will, of course, write you all about us, and tell you all the particulars. Every hour is crowded with incidents, and I have already a very large journal, which increases in size every day. And now Minnie has come, begging the privilege of writing on the back side of my sheet; and you know when she sets out to do any thing, there is no way of denying her; so I will close by subscribing myself, WALTER.

The letter which Minnie wrote will give a little insight into her character, and we present a few passages from it: —

DEAR MAMMA: —

A thousand blessings your little girl sends you, in a letter from this land of promise, where we are stopping. How we got here, what we are doing, and when we leave, prosy Walter will doubtless tell you on the other page. He is the scribe (and sometimes I think the Pharisee) of our party. He moves about among these old tombs, towers, and trumpery with a solemn face, and a note book or portfolio in his hand, taking sketches, and making notes of what he sees and hears, looking gravely at me when I laugh at his enthusiasm, and wondering at my want of appreciation of gravestones and battle fields.

Well, that brother mine is destined for something, and doubtless I am at fault for not being able to enter into his ideas, and sympathizing with his veneration of rust and dust. Perhaps two years — eleven instead of nine — will smooth all the wrinkles out of my face, and make me as demure a little maiden as ever knit stocking, or did crochet work, or pounded a piano.

You need not wonder at my style of writing, for I am changed and grown wild, as Walter says. And no wonder that I should be, travelling with three men, not one of whom feels any interest in fashions or frolics, but who study bridges, shops, cathedrals, and all those things that we ladies feel no special interest in.

And, to confess the truth, I am homesick; I want to see little Charlie, and my dear mamma, and the old friends in Cambridge. Walter acts as if he had no thought of home. However, I expect to be done with all that feeling when we get to London, for Mr. Tenant tells me that homesickness, like seasickness, is to be outlived.

And now the page is full, and I close by sending you a good-night kiss. You may be surprised that I have written such a letter, but, to tell the truth, Mr. Tenant has been looking over my shoulder, telling me what to write — all except the good-night kiss — that was wholly mine.

MINNIE.

"Come, Minnie, it is time for you to retire," said Mr. Percy, entering the room. "And you, Walter, had better fold your letter and send it by the porter to the post office to-night, so that it will be in season for the steamer to-morrow, for your mother would feel badly not to hear from us."

Walter folded the letter carefully, and directed it in a fair, round hand, and ringing the bell for a porter, asked him to take it to the post office, and have it mailed. The porter did as requested, and in a few hours the letter was on its way across the channel. Who can tell the joy it gave to her, who with a mother's patience had remained at home, counting the hours until again she should see her husband and children!

Chapter VIII.

Fancy Trip to Cork.

"Walter, Walter, I thought you were going to get up and see the sun rise," was Minnie's salutation, as she rushed into Walter's apartment, and stood by his bedside.

"Is it morning?" asked Walter, who had been thoroughly jaded out the day before, and who was not astir as early as usual.

"Certainly it is morning, or I should not be here. Come, —

> 'Early to bed, and early to rise,
> Makes a man healthy, wealthy, and wise.'"

"Well, go and arouse father, and order breakfast, and I will soon meet you in the breakfast room."

"Well, don't be all day about it;" and hurrying out of the room, the happy creature was heard singing gayly on her way down to the porter's office.

Soon the whole party were assembled in the breakfast room, and plans were discussed for the day. Mr. Percy thought they could spend the day agreeably and profitably in Dublin, while Mr. Tenant thought best to move on at once towards the south of Ireland.

"We had better start to-morrow morning," remarked Minnie.

"To-morrow is Friday, and that is an unlucky day," said Walter.

"Unlucky day — how silly!" cried Minnie.

"What makes you think Friday is an unlucky day, my son?" asked Mr. Percy.

"I don't know; but every body says so."

"Not every body; superstitious people only believe in lucky and unlucky days."

"Do not more accidents happen on Friday than on any other day?"

"No, I think not. There is no such thing as luck and chance. God rules in the world, and his providence superintends all things. What men call luck is the working of the great plan of Jehovah."

"But I have heard that the day is a very unfortunate one."

"Perhaps you have heard so; and you have heard a hundred other foolish things."

"Friday," added Mr. Tenant, "instead of being an unfortunate day, has been a very fortunate one."

"How so?"

"Because some of the most glorious events of history have taken place on Friday; some of the most useful discoveries have been made on that day."

"In former times, Walter," said Mr. Percy, "there were a great many popular superstitions that sensible people now repudiate."

"Please tell us about them, pa?" shouted Minnie, becoming attentive all at once.

"I have time now only to refer to some of them. It was a common belief, not many years ago, that 'seven' was a charmed number, and that the seventh son would always be fortunate, and that the seventh day of the seventh month would be very fortunate for one born on it; and various other things connected with seven have been stated."

"O, yes, I remember the seventh son — the old doctor that came around a year ago, and cured every body that was sick."

"Professed to be able to cure every body that was sick, my child."

"Yes, that is it; but have any sensible people ever believed that seven was a charmed number?"

"Yes, many of the wisest of the ancients used to believe it, and even Pythagoras, so wise a man, said, in his day, 'Cultivate assiduously the science of numbers. Our vices and our crimes are only errors of calculation.' Some time, children, when we are in the cars, having a long ride, I will tell you about a great many popular superstitions that once were very prevalent, but now are scouted by intelligent men."

It was agreed that they should start, during the day, for the south of Ireland; and Walter was commissioned to go to the office and settle the whole bill for the company, and give notice of the intention to leave the hotel. This he did, counting out the change, which, being in a currency differing from our own, was somewhat difficult.

The party then took a carriage and driver, and leaving the rail cars to go thundering through the land as fast as they could, turned into the Irish highways. travelling very leisurely towards the south. All that day they rode on through a charming country, stopping now and then to converse with the farmers by the roadside, or with the women who sat at the doors of their thatched cottages, spinning or knitting, and at nightfall arrived, after a long ride, at Carrick-on-Suir, in the county of Tipperary. They found a comfortable inn, where they made themselves as happy as possible, and in the evening went out among the houses of the poorer classes of people, who seemed to be quite different from any they had seen in Dublin. They found the town to consist of one long street, running east and west, with several shorter ones diverging from it. Some old ruins were seen, a church in a dilapidated condition, and many poor, mean houses.

The next morning, before breakfast, they all visited the old ruined castle, and wandered through its apartments, and then took a stroll along the winding Suir, which they found to be a very beautiful river. Such healthy exercise gave them a fine appetite for their morning meal, to which they sat down in most excellent spirits. After breakfast a janting car was secured for a ride to Cahir Castle, now in a tolerable state of preservation, and in which Walter became much interested on account of its historical reminiscences. The Earl of Glengall was not at the castle, but a distinguished member of his family received the party with true Irish hospitality, and pointed out to them all the fine views and objects of interest in the vicinity; and it was late in the afternoon ere they reached Clonmell, to which place they went on leaving Cahir. There they stopped all night, meeting with a variety of adventures, which pleased the children very much.

The inn where they lodged was an old-fashioned building, gloomy as one need to see, and not as tidy as the one at Carrick; our friends were subjected to some annoyances which they had not suffered before, and they were not sorry when the time came to leave.

As they rode out, Walter asked his father, "What is the town of Clonmell noted for?"

"For various riotous demonstrations in times past, I believe."

"I think it was the birthplace of Lawrence Sterne," added Mr. Tenant.

"Who was he, Mr. Tenant?" inquired Minnie.

"He was a divine who loved good hunting, and wrote some noted books, among which was Tristram Shandy. His private character did not well qualify him for the holy work to which he was devoted."

"And was not Lady Blessington born here?" asked Mr. Percy.

"I think so," said Mr. Tenant.

The young people were curious to know who Lady Blessington was, and Mr. Tenant gave them several interesting particulars in her history.

They reached Cork at night, and about the first object that arrested the attention of Walter was the old Shandon steeple, a view of which is seen on the next page, and a description of which comes hereafter.

"I'll bet a fig that that steeple has a history which Walter will follow up," said Minnie.

"If it had no history, it would not be an Irish steeple," said Mr. Tenant; "and while we are in Cork, we will see what it is."

They drew up at a fine hotel, where they were soon provided with suitable rooms, at a very moderate charge. Here they remained several days, taking excursions into the country around, visiting the notable buildings in the city, and conversing with the people, who seemed very courteous, and willing to give any information in relation to the history of the city."

"Father," said Walter, "what a funny name this city has! I have been wondering what it was derived from. Do you know?"

"It is said to be derived from *corough,* an old Irish word."

"What does that word *corough* mean?"

"It means a marshy place — a swamp."

"But Cork does not seem to be a marshy place?"

"It does not seem so now. but it once was. It has been drained, and the land raised, and the whole country around has changed."

SHANDON STEEPLE.

Mr. Percy then related to his children some particulars in the history of the city. He told them that " formerly Cork was a very mean city, and quoted what Lord Orrery said to Dean Swift about it in 1736 : 'The butchers are as greasy, the Quakers as formal, and the Presbyterians as holy and as full of the Lord, as ever ; all things are *in statu quo;* even the hogs and pigs grunt in the same cadence as of yore, unfurnished with variety, and drooping under the natural dulness of the place ; materials for a letter are as hard to be found as money, sense, honesty, or truth.' The town was very small then compared with its present growth. Two hundred and fifty years ago it had but one street, and poor at that. It bore all the marks of an Irish village of the lowest stamp, and Camden described it as ' enclosed within a circuit of walls in the form of an egg, with the river flowing round about it, and running between, not passable through but by bridges, lying out in length, as it were, in one direct, broad street, and the same having a bridge over it.'"

The children were very much interested in these statements, and Walter asked " if there had not been some battles fought there in the time of the civil wars in Great Britain."

"I have not time to tell you now about that part of the history of the place. We will find some citizen who knows all about the place, to whom we can apply for facts."

The next morning was the Sabbath, a bright, clear, beautiful day; and while the party were all sitting in one of the parlors of the hotel, looking out upon the crowds that filled the streets, — gayly dressed ladies and men in holiday attire, — the bells on Shandon Steeple sent a merry sound far and wide. Conversation was suspended, as all listened to those harmonious sounds that seemed to be melting on the air, and Walter, as they died away in the distance, repeated a few lines from one of our poets.

> "List the chiming, how it floats
> On the air in tuneful notes!
> List the chiming,
> And the rhyming,
> Of the bells in golden notes.
> So seems to me the poet's art:
> From the music in his heart,
> Words upspringing,
> Widely ringing,
> Are like bell-chimes in the heart.
>
> "Again the chiming, how it floats,
> Now in muffled, mournful notes!
> Slowly tolling,
> Deeply rolling
> On the air in dirge-like notes!

So often seems the poet's art:
From the sorrow in his heart,
  Words revealing
  Depths of feeling
Sound like bell-tolls in the heart."

The mellow sound of these Shandon bells led to a conversation on " bells, bells, brazen bells."

" Where is the largest bell in the world ? " asked Minnie.

" In Russia," said Mr. Percy. " It is called the King of Bells."

" What does it weigh ? "

" It is said to weigh four hundred and forty-three thousand seven hundred and seventy-two pounds, and is more than twenty-one feet high, and if melted up and sold for old metal, would bring three hundred and thirty-two thousand eight hundred and twenty-five dollars. It seems almost incredible, but I have seen the statement gravely put forth, and Walter must look up the facts, and see if what I state on the authority of others is correct."

" Is there any other large bell in Russia ? "

" Yes; the bell on St. Ivan's Church, in Moscow, weighs one hundred and twenty-seven thousand eight hundred and thirty-six pounds, and is of a very rich, superior tone."

" What is the largest bell in England ? "

"I think the one on St. Paul's Cathedral, which you will see when you get to London. The clapper of that weighs one hundred and eighty pounds, and the sides of the bell are more than ten inches thick."

"How can they ring it?"

"They do not ring it, but only use it for tolling on occasions when eminent personages die."

"What does the bell on St. Paul's weigh?"

"As near as I remember, between six and seven tons. There is another at Oxford of about the same size, called 'Great Tom,' which I will take you to see when you reach that interesting old place."

"Have we any bells on the American continent larger than the one on St. Paul's?"

"Yes, the bell at Montreal is said to weigh several tons more."

"I don't see how they get them into the towers."

"That is easily done, my child."

"Do not some of the bells have inscriptions on them?" asked Walter.

"Almost all of them do, my son. They are dedicated to some personage, or the circumstances under which they are cast are stated, or some fancy inscription is put upon them. There is a bell at Rouen, in France, which has an inscription which is thus translated:—

> 'I am George of Ambois—
> Thirty-five thousand in pois;
> But he that will weigh me
> Thirty-six thousand shall find me.'"

Just then the Shandon bells began to ring again, and all paused and listened; and as they closed, Mr. Percy remarked, "There is always something affecting in the sound of a bell, whether it is tolled, or rung, or chimed. I remember of reading a fact which illustrates this. Many years ago, an artist contracted and cast a chime of bells for an Italian convent. The tones were so fine, musical, and melancholy, that all who listened to them, were charmed with the sound. The artist himself was so pleased with his success, that he built a villa near the convent, that he might listen; and there for many years he lived, listening to the music of the bells. But war swept through the valleys and over the mountains of Italy; the monks were scattered, the convent demolished, and the bells carried away; and the artisan, suffering confiscation and persecution, was driven into foreign countries. In course of years, as the story goes, he journeyed to Ireland, and as he sailed in his shallop up the bosom of the broad Shannon, there burst upon his ears a peal of bells from a neighboring cathedral. He had found at last his long-lost treasures, and, bowing his head upon his breast, he listened long in silence. When his companions at length looked towards him, they saw his face still turned to the cathedral; but his eyes had closed forever to this world. He was dead."

"Do you think that is true, father?" asked Minnie.

"I do not know, but I give you the incident just as I read it, and nearly in the author's own language."

The proposal was now made that they go out to church, and on the way pass by Shandon steeple. Walter was disappointed when standing in the street, and looking up into the towering spire, for he expected to see something more elaborate and beautiful. Nor did a glance at the inside increase his admiration. But Mr. Percy reminded him that many buildings in America, for which we have great veneration, are not remarkable for architectural beauty. Faneuil Hall, and the old Independence Hall in Philadelphia, are not the best specimens of art, but they are endeared to the hearts of all who love liberty. And this Shandon steeple is dear to all Corkonians. They have many rich old Irish ballads, in which it finds a central place.

"Can you recite any of these ballads, father?" asked Walter, with earnestness.

"No, but perhaps Mr. Tenant can."

Mr. Tenant, on being thus appealed to, said he could recite a few stanzas of a poem written by a parish priest living near by, which he remembered to have committed to memory long ago.

"Do give them to us," chimed in little Minnie.

Mr. Tenant then recited the following verses, which, he said, were all he could remember of the poem : —

> "I've heard bells chiming
> Full many a clime in,
> Tolling sublime in
>   Cathedral shrine,
> While at a glibe rate
> Brass tongues would vibrate;
> But all their music
>   Spoke nought like thine.
>
> "For memory, dwelling
> On each proud swelling
> Of thy belfry knelling
>   Its bold notes free,
> Made the bells of Shandon
> Sound far more grand on

　　　　The pleasant waters
　　　　　Of the River Lee.

"With deep affection
　And recollection
　I often think of
　　Those Shandon bells,
Whose sounds so wild would,
In the days of childhood,
Fling round my cradle
　　Their magic spells.

"On this I ponder
　Where'er I wander,
　And thus grow fonder,
　　Sweet Cork, of thee;
With thy bells of Shandon,
That sound so grand on
The pleasant waters
　　Of the River Lee."

The whole party attended church in a little chapel built by dissenters, where they heard an earnest, able discourse delivered, by a simple, godly man, to a small, but very devout and sincere audience. The remainder of the day was spent in reading some good books, and seeking spiritual communion with Him who loves the spiritual worshipper.

On Monday, a yacht was engaged, and the travellers took an excursion in the harbor and bay. The day was beautiful, and the whole party was pleased with what they saw. Walter was especially interested, for he found on board the yacht an old man, who stood all day at the helm, with a pipe in his mouth, who was a perfect volume of history, the leaves of which were self-turning; and from him he derived much useful information in relation to Cork and its environs. He also told Walter that many noble and honorable men had lived in or near Cork.

The lad was anxious to know some of them, and the old man mentioned the name of Edmund Spenser.

"Who was he? I never heard of him. Was he a warrior?"

"No, he was an English poet, of considerable note, who became possessor of large tracts of land in Ireland, and took up his residence near Cork."

"What works did he write?"

"He wrote several, among which were the 'Fairy Queen,' the 'View of Ireland,' and some others. But his end was unfortunate."

"Please tell us about it."

"O, well, it is not to the credit of Ireland, but I will tell it. He was a dear, kind, good man, but in an insurrection, with many of which Ireland has been cursed, he was obliged to leave the beautiful house which he had built to be burned by the rioters; and so sudden was his flight, that his infant child was left behind and was burned with the house."

" Did the poet escape ? "

" Yes, he fled into the city, leaving his house burning behind him, and the yells of his pursuers falling on his ears, but found protection here, and finally went to England, and died in sorrow."

" Has Ireland furnished many literary men ? "

" Yes, some of the most distinguished are of Celtic origin. Have you ever heard of Oliver Goldsmith ? He was an Irishman, born in the county of Longford."

" I have read the Vicar of Wakefield, but did not know that Goldsmith was an Irishman," said Minnie.

Mr. Tenant saw the face of the old, weather-beaten sailor lighting up with smiles at the enthusiasm of Minnie, and thought he would touch his pride in another direction; so he said, very quietly,—

" But Goldsmith did not like Ireland; did he ? "

" Sure yes, he would have poured out every drop of his blood for old Ireland."

" But I have read somewhere, that in writing

to a friend, he says, after expressing a wish to see his native land, —

"'But now, to be serious: let me ask myself what gives me a wish to see Ireland again? The country is a fine one, perhaps? No. There is good company in Ireland? No. The conversation there is generally made up, and the vivacity supported, by some humble cousin, who had just folly enough to earn his dinner. Then, perhaps, there's more wit and learning among the Irish? O Lord, no! There has been more money spent in the encouragement of the Padareen mare there in one season, than given in rewards to learned men since the time of Usher. All their productions in learning amount to perhaps a translation, or a few tracts in divinity; and all their productions in wit to just nothing at all. Why the plague, then, so fond of Ireland? Then, all at once, because you, my dear friend, and a few more who are exceptions to the general picture, have a residence there. This it is that gives me all the pangs I feel in separation. I confess I carry this spirit sometimes to the souring of the pleasures I at present possess. If I go to the opera, where Signora Columba pours out all the mazes of melody, I sit and sigh for Lissoy fireside, and Johnny Armstrong's " Last Good Night," from Peggy Golden. If I climb

Hampstead Hill, than where nature never exhibited a more magnificent prospect, I confess it fine; but then I had rather be placed on the little mount before Lissoy gate, and there take in, to me, the most pleasing horizon in nature.'"

The old man heard him repeat the passage, and then exclaimed, —

"No wit among the Irish! That was said after Goldsmith got his Irish heart changed to English."

Walter put one or two more questions, but the old man was wounded, and would not communicate any more information; and Mr. Tenant, to heal the wound that he had made, remarked that it was Goldsmith's life-long wish to return, at last, and die amid the scenes of his boyhood.

"Where did he die?" asked Walter.

"In London, and was buried in the Temple Church, and has a monument to his memory in Westminster Abbey."

The yacht was now nearing the pier, and "all hands," as Walter expressed it, were soon on land.

A little time remaining before nightfall, a visit was made to the Mathew monument, which stands near the Capuchin Church, on Charlotte Quay. Irish gratitude commenced the erection of this memorial of the labors of Father Mathew, who formerly labored here as a priest. The monument is still in an unfinished state. It consists of a double round tower, and when perfected will have an imposing appearance.

"Have you ever seen Father Mathew?" asked Walter of Mr. Percy.

"Yes; ten or twelve years ago he was in America, and I saw him, and heard him speak at one of the Catholic churches in Boston. He also administered the pledge to a large number of people."

Having looked at the monument, walked through some of the streets of Cork, and noticed many features of the style of life among the people, they returned to the hotel, where they took a late dinner, which was prepared for them in excellent style. In the evening Walter and his father went out to present several letters of introduction to distinguished citizens of Cork to whom he had been recommended; and many pleasant interviews they had with fine old Irish gentlemen, who received the strangers with genuine hospitality.

The next morning, Walter, who was the guide and planner for the party, marked out a visit to Blarney Castle, and a janting car was taken for the purpose. The ride was through a fine country, the fields were beautiful with flowers, and the whole face of nature was arrayed in smiles of hopefulness.

Ireland is full of relics; vestiges of ancient Phœnician architecture and life are seen on all sides. The old Druids have left their marks on the very stones of the earth, and the mediæval periods have lingering monuments of their feudal systems, to speak of them to the living age.

Blarney Castle is four miles from Cork, and the road being hard and smooth, the company were soon on the ground. The castle consists of a large square tower and some minor buildings, and is a favorite object with travellers who pass through the south of Ireland.

As they approached it, Mr. Percy told the children that there was a stone in the wall of this Castle which was supposed to have great virtues. Whoever kisses it three times will always succeed in love, will at once become gifted with great powers of persuasion, become an eloquent orator, and receive various other gifts.

"Does any one believe that?" asked Walter.

"It has been believed in times past, and doubtless some superstitious people believe it now. It is said that the Blarney Stone is kissed every year by hundreds of people."

"I'll kiss it," cried Minnie.

BLARNEY CASTLE.

An Irish guide had met them at the gates of the castle, and persisted in showing them through, and at length they came to the part of the edifice that had set in it the wonderful stone. The guide pointed it out. It is in the tower, and he assured Mr. Percy that its merits were not overrated.

Minnie reached up and kissed it, and exclaimed, "Now I shall be an irresistible pleader."

"You talked *blarney* enough before," said Walter.

"But, sure," said the guide to Minnie, "you must kiss it three times."

"Well, three times it is," shouted the enthusiastic child.

"You must go down on your knees."

"Ah, is that it?"

And Minnie complied with all the terms of the superstition, and rattled on so merrily about blarney stones and yielding lovers, that Mr. Percy checked her with the remark, "You are a little too gay, Minnie, and had better reserve some of your remarks until you get home."

The little girl, thus rebuked, became silent, and allowed the guide, in his extravagant way, to describe the wonders of the Blarney Stone.

"I have often heard boys and men say, 'Stop

your blarney,'" said Walter. "Has that any connection with this stone?"

"Yes," said Mr. Tenant; "as this stone is supposed to give readiness of speech to those who kiss it, an excess of talking has been termed 'blarney.'"

"The word never had any significance to me before; now I shall understand it."

"Many words originate in similar ways. Did you ever hear any one term harsh, vile talk, 'Billingsgate'?"

"Yes, sir."

"Well, Billingsgate is a fish market in London, and the fishmongers who deal in the market are very vile tongued, and it has become common to call vile expressions 'Billingsgate' expressions. So an excess of talking is called 'blarney.'"

Having seen the castle, they all rode back to Cork; and as they entered the city, they met a woman in a neat Quaker dress, which led Mr. Percy to remark that in Cork, William Penn, the founder of Pennsylvania, became a Quaker. The children were anxious to know what he was before, and what arguments were used to convert him to the ideas of the Society of Friends.

Mr. Percy told them all he knew about it, which was not much, but enough to satisfy their curiosity.

"When was it?" asked Walter.

"In the year 1658, and the Quakers of that day were not like those of our day. They were more set and rigid."

To illustrate this, he told Walter the story of John Exham, who, about the time of the conversion of Penn, went through the streets of Cork, with sackcloth on his person and ashes on his head, disturbing the people.

"What did they do with him?" asked Minnie.

"They shut him up in prison."

"Was that right, father?"

"No, not unless he disturbed the peace. No error or fanaticism can be put down by persecution."

Thus several days were spent in seeing the objects of interest in the vicinity of Cork. Excursions were made into the country, and many very pleasant places seen. The whole country is rich in historic associations, and Mr. Percy was reluctant to leave, but previously formed plans required it; so they started, at length, for the Lakes of Killarney, in a carriage hired at Cork for the purpose, the driver sitting in front, Mr. Percy and Walter occupying one seat in the vehicle, and Mr. Tenant and Minnie the other.

Chapter IX.

LAKES OF KILLARNEY.

AFTER Walter knew that he was to spend a few months in Europe, he was very apt in forming acquaintance with foreigners; and as Irish people are numerous in Cambridge, he was not put to any inconvenience in getting descriptions of Ireland before he left home. He plagued the Irish servants in the family with questions about the green isle; he talked whole hours with the Irish coachman of one of his father's neighbors, but obtained the most information from a gardener employed by Mr. Tenant.

This gardener was a well-informed man, who had formerly moved in good circles, but who had been reduced by drink, and now labored in a menial service. The old man was born in Killarney, and he was never tired of describing the glories of his native town, and the beautiful lakes. Walter had determined, during these interviews with the gardener, whose name was Patrick Mahoney, to see Killarney Lakes, if he ever lived to tread the soil of Ireland; and when he found himself on his way, he was very happy in the idea that he should see what Pat had so graphically described.

"Patrick, your gardener," said he, turning to Mr. Tenant, "says the lakes are the finest sight he ever saw."

"And Patrick is not alone in that opinion. The great Sir Walter Scott said the same thing, and from what I have read, with some reason, too."

On the arrival of the party at Killarney, they went to the Queen's Hotel, and hired a guide to go with them the next day, which they did very easily, as many persons in the town make a living of conducting strangers to the objects of interest. The town contains about ten thousand inhabitants, and many of them are very poor and illiterate. The Earl of Kenmare owns the whole place, and there is nothing to see there. The principal business is done by hotel keepers, who charge enormous prices for entertaining strangers. If a traveller does not ask for a tariff of prices, and make a definite bargain before he takes his rooms, he is almost sure to be charged at an extravagant rate, whatever may be his accommodations. The hotel season is confined to the few summer months, and the landlords make the most of it. Mr. Percy had guarded against any extortion by fixing the prices to be paid before he had his baggage taken from the carriage. And all travellers in Europe should do this. The consciences of European innkeepers are so elastic that they will cover a most inordinate bill, and the traveller must guard himself by a previous bargain.

When morning came, the whole party started out on their explorations, — Mr. Percy and his friend Tenant on horseback, and Walter and Minnie in a sort of flag-work car, which was drawn by one horse, and rode very easily. We do not expect to follow them in just the course they took, but to refer to the places they visited somewhat briefly, covering a period of three days, which were required to see all the objects of interest.

The lakes are three in number, and into them several small rivers flow continually, and supply them with water. These rivers are the Deenab, the Flesk, the Gearhameen, and several others, scarcely one of which we should dignify with the name of river in this country. The outlet is the River Laune, which connects with the distant sea. These beautiful sheets of water are called the Upper Lake, the Torc Lake, and the Lower Lake, and each one has its objects of interest.

The Upper Lake is two and a half miles long,

and not more than half a mile broad. The scenery around it is very fine, being wild and romantic. As the party came in view of this lake, Minnie shouted with all her might, "Do these people call that a lake?"

"Yes," replied her father, who was riding beside the carriage; "what would you call it?"

"Frog Pond, if we had it on Boston Common."

"It is not its size, but its beauty, my child, that draws attention to it."

"Well, if they make such a fuss over this pond, what would they say if they had Lake Winnipiseogee here in this country?"

"That is right, Minnie; stand up for home," laughingly replied Walter.

"You are a little captious, daughter; this country is unable to suit you."

"No, indeed, pa; but something must be set against Walter's enthusiasm."

On reaching the Upper Lake, they found it to be all that travellers had described it to be; its banks set with the beautiful *arbutus unedo;* and waters dashing now on a sandy shore, and anon against the base of the high cliff, and beautiful landscape views breaking upon the sight in all directions.

The Torc Lake is about two miles long, and

half as wide. One or two villages are on its banks, objects of interest are seen in all directions, and the islands dotting the lake appear like green clumps of grass rising above the surface of the water. It is charming to ride along the lake, or to sail across it; and as Minnie stood, getting one view after another, she began to confess the charm which the scenery exercised upon her.

The Lower Lake is the largest of the three, and is more tame in its scenery, having around it fewer of the wild scenes which distinguish the others. Our party staid long enough around them to get a view of all the objects of interest, and see all the famous landscape scenes. The view which charmed Walter most was from the summit of Torc Mountain. After a climb which to the children was very laborious, they found themselves on the top. As they stood there they saw a river flowing between it and the neighboring mountain, and Walter asked,—

"What mountains are those in the distance?"

"That beyond the river is the Mangerton Mountain; on the other side of us are the Glena Mountains."

"How high is this one, pa?" asked Minnie.

"About eighteen hundred feet."

The view from the summit of this mountain

was a delightful one, and for a long time they stood enjoying it. After partaking of some refreshments on the Torc, they descended, which was about as difficult a thing to do as the ascent, so precipitous and uneven are the sides of the hill.

As they came down they visited the Torc Waterfall, a beautiful cascade that dashes down over the sultry rocks, now almost hidden beneath the foliage, and anon splashing on, casting up beautiful spray,—roaring, and foaming, and tumbling down the cliffs, now in one broad sheet, and anon broken and shivered into little spiteful jets.

They came in sight of Muckross Abbey, an old ruin, with a choir window yet in a state of considerable perfection, and a square tower, broken at the top, and hung with vines that are creeping over it. It was formerly a Franciscan monastery; but the monks died long ago, and the edifice where once they counted their beads, and chanted their prayers, is now a mass of ruins. The guide told Walter that the abbey was founded in the year 1440, and that hundreds of years before that a church stood on this spot.

"Will you see the Lady's Walk?" asked the guide.

"Where is that?" inquired Minnie.

They entered a fine walk, which leads from the abbey along the shores of the lake, beside which seats are placed for the accommodation of those who wish to rest and meditate on the sober reminiscences of the place. The Walk is two or three miles long, but our party did not pursue it far. He also pointed them to the trunk of the yew tree to which Inglis alludes in the following passage: "No one should visit Killarney without seeing Muckross Abbey. It is a very beautiful and very perfect remain, and contains within it the most gigantic yew tree I have ever seen; its arms actually support the crumbling wall, and form a canopy above the open cloisters. The trunk of this majestic yew tree measures thirteen feet in circumference."

On Dinis Island they dined. There is on this island an elegant little cottage, where substantial refreshments are kept for visitors. Another party had just left the cottage, and our friends took their places at the table. A moderate bill of fare was put before them; and at Walter's order, a fine dish of boiled salmon was brought on, and with the other accompaniments, a nice, wholesome, though frugal, meal was made. The island is connected with the main land by a little bridge on one side, and with

Brickeen Island in the same way on the other side. After dinner the party went out and threw themselves on the greensward, and conversed of home and friends for a long time.

Having rested, they proceeded to the Eagle's Nest, a curious hill, conical in form. It has a flat, bare top, while its sides are all covered with beautiful shrubbery.

"Shall we climb the mountain?" asked Mr. Percy.

"I do not care about it," said Mr. Tenant.

"O, do go up; I am not tired," was Minnie's answer.

"Yes, I want to go up," said Walter.

"Two against one," said Mr. Percy, "and I also incline to see the top."

So they all started on, parting the shrubbery, and wandering among the trees, and after a very bold climbing, reached the summit. Here Walter asked, —

"Why is this elevation called the Eagle's Nest?"

"Because," replied his father, "in the rocks around us the eagles build their nests."

"I do not see any signs of eagles."

"No, they are not so common here as formerly. Since visitors have come to the mountain and lakes in such vast numbers, the retreat of the eagles has been disturbed."

On descending from the mountain, the guide took a pistol from his pocket, at the sight of which Minnie started.

"What are you going to do with that?"

"You will see," he replied.

"I guess I know," said Walter.

"What, what? tell me," was Minnie's impatient rejoinder.

"I think he is going to shoot an eagle."

"Where is the eagle?"

"I do not see him, but perhaps the guide does."

Mr. Percy was as much at a loss to know what the fellow was about to do as his children were, nor was Mr. Tenant any better informed. But the matter was soon explained, for the guide discharged the pistol into the air. For a moment after the report all was still; then a single echo, and then another, and another, until the whole mountain seemed to be full of unseen shooters. The effect was so grand that the children clapped their hands in the greatest glee, and, at the earnest solicitation of the gentlemen, the pistol was discharged again with greater effect than before. The party then descended, very rapidly, the Long Range, and passed under the old Weir

Bridge, which, with two spans, crosses the stream, which is very rapid. Minnie, who is not very timid, was actually frightened as the boat went whirling along by the stones, and dashing on through dangers which would have appalled persons of a more advanced age. The little girl said nothing, but her pale face and compressed lips showed how much her fears were aroused. When the boat shot out into Muckross Lake, she breathed freely, exclaiming, —

"I am glad that is over!"

The next day they visited several places, among which was Ross Island, on which stands the ruins of Ross Castle. Concerning this castle there are many strange tales of horror, which the guide related to the children, who treasured every one of them. Some of them were so absurd, that they made much sport for the young people. They went through the castle, and ascended to the top of the square tower, from which point a fine view of the country was obtained.

As they came down, the guide told Walter of a famous echo, at the base of this huge tower. He told him that there was a legend, which affirmed that a giant named Paddy Blake, was concealed under the tower, and that whoever called to him would receive an answer. Walter called, as the guide told him to, and a hoarse sound was the response; and Minnie declared that if that was the giant's answer, it was not very intelligible; and Walter assured the guide that he had not much faith in Paddy Blake.

As they wandered about the island, they found some evidences of the fact that the copper mining had been carried on in the place. It seems that about fifty years ago, a few gentlemen endeavored to reopen the mine on this island, which had been worked a great many years before. They toiled on a while, and when the prospect of the mine became very profitable, the water from the lake broke in, and the operation will probably never be resumed.

The three days were taken up in visits to the various objects of interest around the lakes. They saw the famous Logan Stone, left by the ancient Druids to puzzle and perplex the curious; the Devil's Punch Bowl, not half so dangerous as the common punch bowl, though a very wild place; the Gap of Dunloe, a sort of Alpine pass, though found in Ireland; and many other interesting things and places. They stood and looked up upon O'Sullivan's Falls, and wandered into O'Sullivan's Grotto; they wandered about Dunloe Castle, charmed with its stern, wild appearance; and saw every thing from O'Donoghue's prison to his pulpit, and returned to Killarney with a most delightful impression of the lakes and the mountains.

The morning after, it was arranged to journey north, by early stages, and see the country, and get what information they could concerning the habits and customs of the people. For this purpose they took a carriage, seating four persons besides the driver, and started out, as they had come to Killarney. As they rode on, Mr. Tenant asked Walter what he should tell Patrick Mahoney about the lakes of Killarney.

"I shall tell him they are all he described them to be."

"Then you are not disappointed?"

"Not at all."

"Nor I," said Minnie. "These lakes are beautiful."

And this was the general expression, Mr. Percy uniting in praise of the beautiful scenery as earnestly as his children.

As they rode on, the children were amused with many things which they saw. A boy driving a donkey, with two baskets over his back, one hanging down on each side, made much sport for Minnie. An old farmer, driving his wife and child along the road in a basket-work carriage, drawn by a horse that looked as if he had been fed on sawdust, (a view of which we give on the next page,) also drew their attention. They were also much pleased with the abbeys and ruins of churches which were seen all along the way through the country; and Mr. Percy gave to his children such facts in relation to these ruined edifices, as made even the frolicking Minnie to look upon them with interest. He related; as they rode on, many interesting legends; for almost all the old ruins have curious tales to tell.

"You remember," he said to Walter, "an old abbey we saw on the banks of the Suir?"

"Certainly, sir."

"What, father, the Holy Cross Abbey?" asked Minnie.

"Yes, my child."

"Why is it called by this name?" asked Walter. "I forgot to ask at the time."

"It was so called, I believe, because in the year 1110, Pope Pascal sent to the church connected with the abbey a piece of the true cross: and it was to speak of this circumstance that I called your attention to the abbey."

"Was it a piece of the true cross?"

"Of course not. I have seen in Europe many pieces of wood which were said, by super-

IRISH RIDING.

stitious people, to be pieces of the true cross; but they were miserable impositions."

"What became of the piece of wood that was sent by the pope to this abbey?"

"It was set in gold and precious stones, and for a long time venerated by the people; but what has become of it I do not know."

Mr. Percy then gave many interesting reminiscences of the abbey, (for a view of which see the frontispiece to this volume,) and the children were delighted with the entertainment.

They rode in a northerly direction until they struck a railroad, where they dismissed their carriage and driver, and proceeded by rail to Dublin, having had a most interesting tour in the south of Ireland.

"How long do you stay here?" asked Walter of his father on the evening of their arrival.

"Only one night, my son. To-morrow we will go out to Maynooth, and then proceed towards the north."

Accordingly they bade adieu to Dublin, and proceeded to Maynooth, on the way to the interesting places in the north of Ireland, where they were to stay for a few days before crossing over to Scotland.

Chapter X.

MAYNOOTH AND DROGHEDA.

"And is this Maynooth, of which I have heard and read so much?" asked Walter, as they entered that town.

"I suppose it is. But what have you heard or read about it, Walter?" asked Mr. Percy.

"I have read of Maynooth College, and have seen in the English papers signs of strife between the friends and foes of the college."

"Why should there be a strife about a college?" asked Minnie.

"Because," replied her father, "this college is for the education of young men for the Roman Catholic priesthood, and Protestants oppose all grants of money, on the ground that it is a sectarian institution."

"But are not all the English colleges as sectarian?" asked Walter.

"They are most of them under the control of the Church of England."

"Then where is the difference?"

"The difference consists in the fact that while

in English colleges, generally, young men are educated for all professions and vocations in life, and the theological training is not made a specality; in Maynooth the young men are trained directly for the priesthood."

"Then the college is more like the Andover Seminary, or the institution at Newton?"

"It is an institution lying between the college and the theological seminary, or rather combining both."

"When was this college founded?"

"In the year 1795."

Thus conversing, they reached the college, and Mr. Percy having a letter of introduction to one of the prominent teachers, the whole party were very kindly received, and shown through the buildings, which are very finely located, and very spacious. They consist of chapel, dormitories, lecture and recitation rooms, professors' apartments, library, dining halls, and all the usual conveniences of such an institution.

When they had inspected the college buildings, one of the professors very kindly accompanied them to the parish church, a building of some historical interest, to the old ruined castle of the Fitzgeralds, built several centuries ago, and to all the various objects of interest in the town. Of the latter there were, indeed, few, as the town of Maynooth is small, and has only one principal street, and few buildings of importance except those mentioned.

As the day advanced, they took the cars for Drogheda, where they decided to spend the night. While waiting in the station house, Walter proposed to ride in the third-class cars.

"We have been riding in the first-class cars, and we have seen nobody but ourselves," he said. "We have a whole car to ourselves, and do not see the people as I would like to see them."

"A sensible suggestion," replied Mr. Tenant; "and as the distance to Drogheda is short, I propose that we follow Walter's advice."

"But Minnie will be most inconvenienced. If she consents, I have no objection," said Mr. Percy; "but she must remember that she will be crowded into a car with many very dirty people, some of whom will be smoking, and some swearing, and some yelling."

"What say, Minnie?" asked Walter.

"I say yes," replied the little girl; "I dare go any where that you dare carry me."

So it was agreed that they should take the third-class cars, and the tickets were purchased accordingly.

On entering the car, they found it filled with

a very rough looking set of people. The seats were close together, the windows were small, and the prospect of a pleasant ride not altogether auspicious. The Irish peasants, who filled the carriage, conversed boisterously together, and Minnie began to regret that they had taken their tickets in the third class. But a humorous remark, indulged in by a full-faced, genial old man, at the expense of a fellow-traveller, provoked shouts of laughter, in which our friends joined, and the whole company soon became very much interested in the wit and fun for which the Irish people are noted.

Mr. Percy soon engaged in conversation with some of the men, who were very communicative, furnishing all the information in their power in relation to the country through which they were riding, the politics and morals of the people, and the religious condition and prospects of the Irish nation. Walter was delighted with the country, all waving with grain, beautiful to the eye, fragrant and fair, and reminding one of the beauties of Eden. He could scarcely restrain his emotions as one view after another burst upon him, and in his enthusiasm, he forgot his hard seat and uncouth fellow-passengers, absorbed in the landscape scenes, which every where presented themselves. Minnie was amusing herself with the quaint remarks, the curious pronunciation, and the general hilarity of the Irish people in the car, and she laughed as heartily, if not as boisterously, as they. Mr. Tenant, with his cigar in his mouth, sat leaning back in a corner, now and then uttering some remark, to add to the general good feeling which seemed to exist, himself pleased that he could be in a company that were not annoyed by his bad habit of smoking — a habit which he unfortunately contracted when a boy, but which strengthened with his strength and grew with his growth.

"How is it," asked Walter, " that a country which looks so fertile, and has so many evidences of thrift, can contain so many poor people?"

Mr. Percy explained, and gave his son much useful information in relation to the way in which the lands in Ireland are held, the tenantry system, and the various causes which tend to the poverty of the laboring classes.

Thus they rode on, passing several interesting Irish towns, (one of which appears on the opposite page,) with their humble church, lowly graveyard, thatched and stone cottages, and their poor but cheerful inhabitants; and when the children found the cars had reached Drogheda, they complained that the ride was so short,

AN IRISH TOWN.

and that they were so soon to part company with those who had furnished them so much amusement and information.

"What a wonderful way of travelling we have!" said Walter; "and how surprised our ancestors would be if they could come back from their graves, and see steam carriages flying across the country as rapidly as we have come from Maynooth!"

"Yes, my son," replied Mr. Percy, "in nothing do we see greater improvements than in the facilities for travelling. Stage coaches were introduced into England about the year 1670, to take the place of private carriages, post chaises, and saddle riding; and now we have locomotives instead of horses, and beautiful cars instead of the awkward vehicles which then went over the road, about thirty miles per day."

"Where did the first stage coach run — over what road?"

"From Oxford to London. It was called the Flying Coach."

"I suppose the people then thought that as wonderful as we now think the railway is?"

"Yes, it was an enterprise so important that the University of Oxford gravely considered it, and issued a recommendatory notice of it; but many people opposed it as a dangerous innovation."

"A dangerous innovation?"

"Yes, a tract was published against it, and hundreds of people petitioned the king that certain restrictions might be put upon it. These restrictions, which related to its speed, the frequency of the passages, the number of horses to be attached to it, the petitioners hoped would make the stage coach so unprofitable that few would feel desirous of sustaining it."

"What objection could they have to such an improvement in the mode of travelling?"

"They had various objections, all of which were unsound and frivolous. Mr. Macaulay tells us that it was vehemently 'argued that this mode of conveyance would be fatal to the breed of horses and the noble art of horsemanship; that the Thames, which had long been an important nursery of seamen, would cease to be the chief thoroughfare from London up to Windsor and down to Gravesend; that saddlers and spurriers would be ruined by hundreds; that numerous inns, at which mounted travellers had been in the habit of stopping, would be deserted, and would no longer pay any rent; that the new carriages would be too cold in winter and too hot in summer; that the passengers would be grievously annoyed by invalids and crying children; that the coach would sometimes reach the inn so late that the passengers could get no supper, and start so early in the morning that they could get no breakfast.'"

The cars now stopped at Drogheda, and our company at once repaired to the hotel, an old-fashioned, comfortable inn. This Drogheda is a very interesting old Irish town, which has a memorable history, and our friends were very much interested in visiting it. The place has about thirty thousand inhabitants; the streets remind one of the middle ages; the houses are peculiar and odd, the citizens seem like a different race; and every aspect of the place is interesting and unfamiliar.

Having left their carpet bags at the inn, they went out to see the town. On passing along, they noticed, not far from the centre of the place, a huge square tower, and on inquiry, were told that it was "Magdalen's Steeple." It is a very high, venerable tower, in which the bats have made their abode, and which looks as if it might soon tumble to the ground. When it was built, no one can tell. The church of which it was once the tower fell down four hundred years ago, and this memorial of it still bears the pelting of the storms, and feels from year to year the crumbling hand of time passing over it.

The children were much amused in visiting

some of the cabins of the poor people, and we give Walter's idea of them in an extract from his journal.

DROGHEDA.

After viewing " Magdalen's Steeple," we went to see some of the houses of the poor people on the outskirts of the town. As one of them will answer for a description of the whole, I will write it out in my journal. We went into the one I am about to describe, and found it occupied by an elderly woman, her son, and daughter. The building was not one of the poorest kind, which are generally built of turf, but was of a better class, built of rough stone, unhewn, and without any claim to taste or elegance. The stone walls were whitewashed within and without. The building was an oblong, thirty feet long, and fifteen feet wide. The roof was thatched with straw, the thatching being about one foot thick. The straw is carefully laid upon small poles which serve for rafters, and will last six or eight years.

The interior of the house was divided into two apartments by a curtain about eight feet high, thus making two rooms about fifteen feet square. The windows were fixed in the stonework, and could not be moved. The glass was about five inches square, and the whole window about eighteen inches square. The floor was the bare ground, beaten hard, cold and damp. The chimney and fireplace were at one end, built of stone and clay, a mere rough pile to hold the fire and conduct the smoke into the outer region. A loom for the manufacture of Irish linen was in one room, and the young woman was at work upon it. The adornments of the cabin were very few; the women were barefoot; the whole aspect of the house cheerless and dreary, much resembling the cells of a prison. And yet every thing was neat and tidy, and the people seemed to be quite happy. The old lady received us very kindly, and answered the questions we asked with much intelligence, and was much gratified with our visit.

When she found we were Americans, she said, "Then you know my sister's boy, Mike O'Brien, who lives over there."

Father told her he had never seen him, at which she seemed surprised, exclaiming, —

"What, you come from America, and never saw Mike O'Brien!"

"Where does he live?" asked father.

"In Wisconsin, sure."

We told her that we lived a great distance from Wisconsin, and that we never had been there; but she could not comprehend the vastness of our country.

The town of Drogheda has a solemn and fearful history. It held out for a long time against Cromwell, who poured his vengeance out upon it until the streets ran with blood. September 3, 1649, he encamped on the neighboring hills, and began to fortify them. Within the town the brave Ormond had placed his choicest soldiers and his heaviest cannon, and deemed his defences impregnable. For six days did the Protector fortify the distant hills, and at the end of that time hoisted his red flag, and poured his iron rain upon the doomed place beneath him. The siege continued until Drogheda was one vast pile of ruins, one general receptacle of death. The streets flowed with blood; calls for mercy were heard in vain; hundreds, driven into the churches, were burned there, and in the houses were heard sounds of lamentation and sorrow. So dreadful was the massacre, and so deep the rivers of blood, that all Ireland was overwhelmed with consternation. Cromwell seemed to be writing his edicts in great letters of blood, and the cold chill of horror ran through the whole land.

From Drogheda, our friends made an excursion out to the field where was fought the battle of the Boyne; and Walter listened with much interest as his father described the battle which was fought in 1690 by the armies of James II. and William III.

"Which was victorious?" he asked.

"William gained the day."

"And what became of James?"

"His army was routed, and he fled into England."

Mr. Percy explained the relations which existed between these two warriors, and the causes which induced them to fight with each other; and every young reader will find it interesting to turn to the history of those times, and read what is written of the battle of the Boyne.

The party left Drogheda for Belfast, stopping at Dundalk, Newry, Armagh, and several other interesting towns, on the way, in each of which they saw something new, and became better acquainted with the Irish people.

Chapter XI.

GLANCES AT GIANT'S CAUSEWAY.

"BELFAST! passengers for Belfast stop here!" shouted the conductor as the train stopped in the station house of that city.

The party at once sought lodgings, and then made arrangements at once to visit that interesting natural phenomenon, the Giant's Causeway, on the north coast of Ireland, and the rugged scenery of Donegal and Antrim. They took a jaunting car, and pursued the road along the coast, by the Lough of Belfast, with the heaving sea in view much of the distance. After riding through a country beautifully picturesque, they reached the Causeway, pictures of which Walter had often seen.

They found many persons waiting and desiring to act as guides, each professing to be better acquainted with the scenery than the others. The privilege of selecting a guide from all these was left to Walter, who ran his eye over the crowd, and with considerable intuitive discernment, made choice of a lad a few years older than himself, with a bright eye, and a garb peculiar to his class. He may be seen in the accompanying engraving, with Walter's umbrella and Minnie's cloak, standing at the Giant's Well.

THE GUIDE AT GIANT'S WELL.

This guide led them forth to the Pleaskin, the Grand Causeway, which consists of a very curious combination of crystallized rocks, which are thus described:—

" These remarkable specimens of nature's

handiwork are of unequal height and breadth. They rise up from the strand to a height of about twenty feet, gradually receding to the water; though how far seaward this arrangement extends is very uncertain. This grand assemblage of basaltic pillars extends for a considerable distance along the shore; sometimes like a vast pile congregated together, as in the Grand Causeway; sometimes taking the shape of isolated masses of broken, disjointed rocks scattered along the beach; sometimes assuming the appearance of regular geological strata in the exposed face of the cliff, as in that remarkable natural curiosity, the 'Giant's Organ;' and sometimes becoming part of the rugged mountainous coast itself, as in the headland known as the 'Chimney Tops.' But in whatever part of the coast these basaltic pillars appear, they have all two peculiarities — their almost uniform pentagonal figure, and the singular manner in which the separate pieces of each column are jointed together. In no cases do the columns seem to consist of single solid blocks, but are composed of a number of short lengths, one on the top of the other, like layers of masonry. But instead of possessing flat surfaces, the ends of each length are articulated one into the other like a ball and socket, in the same way as is observable in the vertebræ of some of the larger kinds of fishes — the one end of the joint having a cavity into which the convex end of the opposite exactly fits. The depth of this concavity or convexity is generally about three or four inches; and it is peculiar that the joint, instead of being conformable to the external angular figure of the block, is exactly round, and as large as the diameter of the column will admit; consequently, as the angles of these columns are in general very unequal, the circular edges of the joints are seldom coincident with more than two or three sides of the pentagon, and are, from the edge of the circular part of the joint to the exterior sides and angles, quite plain. The articulations of these joints are frequently inverted, in some of them the concavity being upwards, and in others the reverse. This occasions that variety and mixture of concavities and convexities on the tops of the columns which is observable throughout the platform of this Causeway without any discoverable design or regularity with respect to the number of either."

The effect of this view upon our travellers was impressive, and they stood, for a long time, viewing the wonderful work of God.

"These rocks look like chimneys," said Minnie.

"Very much so," replied Mr. Tenant.

"They are sometimes mistaken for chimneys," said the guide, who told them that on one occasion a Spanish ship mistook them for the towers and chimneys of Dunluce Castle, which is near by, and wasted considerable ammunition by firing into them.

GIANT'S GATEWAY.

Minnie laughed heartily at this mistake.

The party then went through the Giant's Gateway, a view of which is given in the engraving.

"This is the way the giants used to enter the Causeway," said the guide.

"You do not mean that giants ever lived here; do you?" asked Minnie.

"Who, then, could have formed this Gateway?"

"The great God," replied the child.

The guide then took them to the "Lady's Chair," which he said was used by the queen of the giants.

"She must have been a large woman," said Walter.

"Giants usually are large," replied the guide.

"She must have loved a hard seat," said Minnie.

This Chair consists of a number of huge basaltic stones put together, forming a mammoth chair, or seat; and when Walter saw it, it was overhung with beautiful vines, and decorated with humble flowers, that found a place to grow between the stones, and bore a striking resemblance to a huge chair, worthy of a giantess.

The Giant's Well is partly natural, and partly artificial, and the water is pure and pleasant to the taste. A distinguished visitor to the spot says, "The only person I observed on the Causeway, when I descended, was an old woman sitting by the spring of fresh water, with a whiskey bottle and glasses to mix that national spirit with the pure spring, and render it more palatable to her customers. On returning from my ramble, however, I perceived a young lady, in a riding habit, sitting down by the side of the fountain, waiting the return of some gentlemen who were examining the Causeway; the sight of whom, in this lonely spot, I am free to confess, drove all the pentagons and hexagons out of my head; and to escape from the chance of its being filled with something else, I was ungallant enough to take an abrupt departure."

"Do you not suppose this Causeway was formed by human hands?" asked Walter of his father, as they wandered from point to point.

"No, my son, there is no chance for such a supposition."

"Why not, father?"

"Because, in the first place, there could be no conceivable object for such a structure; and second, because the rocks are so dissimilar, and are so unlike what man would form, that the idea can hardly be seriously entertained for a moment."

"But look at the regularity of the stones, as they lie together; that indicates art."

"At the first glance it looks like it; but if

these pillars were made from a pattern, they would bear a more striking likeness to each other."

"Do they not all look alike?"

"Yes, just as the leaves are alike in general construction, but endlessly diverse; just as all human faces are alike, but all of them possessed of an individual identity."

"I understand."

"Notice, Walter, that all these pieces of stone are so different, that they could not be worked from any one pattern."

"Yes, but is there no other reason?"

"Several I might mention. The extent of these hexagonal, octagonal, pentagonal, and nonagonal, found all along the coast of Antrim and Donegal, shows that they were cast up by Nature in some one of her freaks."

"Well, father, you must explain those hard words you have just used. I do not understand them," said Minnie.

"What words, my daughter?"

"Why, hexagonal — what is that?"

"Hexagonal, my child, means having six sides and angles, as you see some of these stones have."

"What are the octagonal stones?"

"Those having eight sides and angles."

"And how many angles have the pentagonal?"

"Five."

"And what are the — the nonagonal, I believe you called it?"

"Those that have nine sides and angles."

The guide secured a six-oared row boat, and took the party out upon the water, where they could have a very fine view of the whole Causeway; and as they rowed about, Walter opened his guide book, and read aloud the following testimony to the effect produced upon the mind by looking upon this grand natural wonder: "What shall I say of the Causeway?" inquires Lord John Manners. "There are three promontories running into the sea on a level with the waves, or nearly so, composed of upright blocks of stone, each, it may be, a yard in circumference, hexagonal, pentagonal, octagonal, and one or two nonagonal in shape; some of the cliffs, too, are fluted in this manner, with columns thirty feet high, resembling, at a little distance, the pipes of an organ. A very steep and narrow track took us from the Causeway to the summit of the cliffs — an ascent of about three hundred feet, and a walk of a couple of miles along their edge to the Pleaskin Rock. It rained furiously, so that it was only now and then we could obtain a fair view of the dark creeks, and bold rocks, and strange formations of whinstone, which diversify this mysterious coast."

"How fortunate we are that we have not a rainy day now!" said Minnie.

"We shall get from the water here the favorite view of travellers — the sunset view."

"Is that a better view than any other?" asked Walter.

"It is said to be so; and travellers, who have time to do so, tarry, and behold these huge rocks, towers, and chimneys, lighted up and gilded by the last rays of the descending sun."

"We shall soon test it, for the sun is descending fast."

"See, father," cried Minnie, "how red the western sky looks. O, how beautiful the colors that glow, and change, and disappear."

Walter, and the whole company, turned towards the west, and all admired the gorgeous drapery that old Sol had wrapped about his royal person as he retired to rest; and they sat silent in their boat, waiting for the beams to strike the pinnacles above them.

And they waited not long, for the sun, like a great red orb, went rolling down behind the hills, flinging its parting beams on the Causeway, gorgeously lighting and shading its pinnacles, and bringing out the bold outlines of the countless columns; and the children shouted with joy as they witnessed the changing aspects of the dwelling place of the giants; and as they rowed rapidly to the shore, Walter repeated, from memory, the lines of one of our poets, written after viewing this wonderful mass of pillared stone: —

> "Dark o'er the foam-white waves,
> The Giant's Pier the war of tempests braves —
> A far-projecting, firm, basaltic way
> Of clustering columns wedged in dense array;
> With skill so like, yet so surpassing art,
> With such design, so just in every part,
> That reason pauses, doubtful if it stand
> The work of mortal or immortal hand."

That night they found lodgings at the village of Ballinatoy, at an inn, where several parties, who, like themselves, had come to visit the Causeway, had taken refuge. Walter sought the public room, where were villagers, guides, and strangers, talking about the Causeway, and relating to each other the fables and legends connected with the place.

He was told that, a year before, a young American lady had seated herself in the Lady's Chair, and remained so long that she took a violent cold, and came back to this hotel, sickened, and died. The superstitious people in the vicinity believe that in some way she offended the spirit of the giants, who still hover around the ruins of their ancient home, and that they smote her with death.

A guide also related to him the story of a young lady, who, several years ago, climbed out upon these rocks to get a leaf that was growing in a crevice of the ledge, when the basaltic stones beneath her feet became disturbed, and she was plunged down the cliff, and taken up by her friends a lifeless form.

As the evening advanced, the weary party sought repose, and soon the children were asleep, dreaming of giants, castles, and banditti, living over in sleep the events and legends of the day.

Chapter XII.

DUNLUCE CASTLE.

Ding — dong — ding!   Ding — dong — ding!

"What is that?" shouted Minnie to Walter, running from her little bedroom into the chamber where her brother slept.

"What is it? Why, breakfast time, to be sure."

"Then this is the first time we have heard a bell ring for breakfast. I thought they had no public table."

"You thought!"

"Yes, I thought, and believe I am right, though it sounds much like our bell at home."

"You will find the bell to be a call to the breakfast table."

At this moment Mr. Percy entered Walter's room, and once more the children both asked, "What was that bell for?"

"It was rung for the passengers who are going to Belfast in a stage that is about starting to get ready."

"Do we go in it?" asked Minnie.

"No, my daughter."

"O, why not! I love to go in a crowd."

"Because we are not ready to go. We have had no breakfast, and your toilet is not completed; and then we go to Dunluce Castle to-day."

The crack of the driver's whip, the rumbling of wheels, the shout of the passengers, announced that the stage had started."

After breakfast, in a janting car our friends rode out to Dunluce Castle. The ride was a short one, and intensely interesting; and all were sorry when the old frowning towers were reached, so much did they admire the scenery of the shore road along which they travelled.

Dunluce Castle is rather a remarkable structure, which has been well described as "the grandest, romantickest, awfullest sea-king's castle in broad Europe. It stands on a great ledge of a cliff, separated from, rather than joined to, the main land by the narrowest of natural bridges, and overhangs the sea — that dark, chilling, northern sea — so perpendicularly, that how the towers and wall on the seaside were built I cannot divine: what numbers of masons and builders must have fallen into that gloomy sea before the last loophole was pierced! The landward scenery, in spite of good roads and modern improvements, is dreary enough now; what it must have been when those grim halls were first inhabited by Ulster chieftains, who can guess? There is no castle on the Rhine, or the Loire, or the Seine, or any where else that I know of, that can be compared with Dunluce for desolate, awe-inspiring grandeur."

The travellers crossed a narrow rock which serves for a bridge, and entered the gloomy castle. They were met by a porter who conducted them through it. What pleased Walter most was the fine views obtained from the lofty towers. But Minnie was most interested in some wild tales which the porter related as they went from room to room. "Here," said he, "in this apartment, sickened and died a beautiful and gifted lady, who was brought here by the former lord of the castle."

"Please tell me about her," cried Minnie.

"Be patient, little lady, and I will."

"Patience is not a virtue when I want to hear a story," laughingly replied the little girl.

The guide went on with his tale. He told them that many years ago the lord of this castle became enamoured of a beautiful woman, who lived about one hundred miles away. She did not favor his suit, and gave her hand to another. But the knight, enraged at his want of success, gathered a number of faithful servants, and coming at night upon the castle where she lived, took her away, and brought her to Dunluce Castle. The costliest decorations and the most beautiful furniture were used for her chamber, and every attention was paid to her wants; but in a few weeks, finding escape impossible, she sickened, and one morning, when the knight came to press his suit, he found the lady on her knees, her hands clasped, and her eyes fixed upon a crucifix before her. Supposing she was at her devotions, and not wishing to disturb her, he returned. In an hour he came again, and found her still on her knees. He touched her, and she moved not, answered not. He bent down, and looked in her pale but still beautiful face, and started back with horror. She was dead."

"Dead!" exclaimed Minnie.

"Yes, her spirit had fled from earth."

"What did they do with the wicked man?"

"Nothing at all. The state of society was very different then from now, and he was a man of great power."

"Well, what else about it?"

"O, nothing; only it is supposed that the

spirit of this lady sometimes visits this room at night, and —— "

"O, what nonsense! It seems as if the people of this country believed in nothing but ghosts and hobgoblins."

"I was telling you what some suppose, and what not a few seriously believe."

"I am glad," said Mr. Percy, "that my daughter discredits all such stories. They are absurd and very ridiculous, and are only fit to be laughed at and scorned."

The whole company were delighted with the romantic scenery in the vicinity of the castle, rendered interesting by the huge masses of basaltic rock, which can be seen in all directions; and the whole day was spent in looking over the grounds, and wandering about the castle. Walter scratched his name on one of the stones of the tower, nearly spoiling a new knife in doing it; and doubtless whoever visits the castle in future will be able to find it: —

WALTER PERCY.
ANNO DOMINI MDCCCLVIII.

On returning to Belfast, Walter wrote a description of his visit to the Giant's Causeway, and sent it to Charlie. It read as follows: —

Brother Charlie: —

You remember to have seen in some of your books a picture of the Giant's Causeway, a remarkable object of interest in the north of Ireland. Well, your sister Minnie and myself have been to visit it, and a wonderful place it is. A beautiful lad, little older than I am, was our guide, and we paid him for his services two days, three dollars. He wore a little red knit cap, a light velvet jacket, and looked trim and neat, as he ran on before us, or turned, his face all glowing with smiles, to point out the objects of interest.

I cannot tell you all we saw, the objects were so numerous. The guide took us to the Lady's Chair, in which the giant's wife used to sit; to the well of which the giants drank; to the mighty Causeway itself, a natural wonder, such as you never saw.

With all these objects Minnie as well as myself were delighted, and father allowed us to purchase several fine views of the Causeway and Dunluce Castle, which is near by, and we shall bring them home for you to look at, though you are such a little boy that we do not expect you will be as much interested in them as you are in your new rocking horse.

Father says that when you become a large

boy he will take you across the ocean to see the very objects we have visited to-day. Then you will be able to understand and enjoy them as we do now.

And now, Charlie, I hope you take good care of Rover; give him enough to eat, and do not play too hard with him. Do not get into any mischief yourself, and be a very good boy, and when we return we will tell you all we have seen. I shall be delighted to sit down evenings in our happy home in Cambridge, and tell you all about the places we have visited, the people with whom we have conversed, and the incidents with which we have met.

It is now ten o'clock, and father says I must retire; and so I bid you good night.

WALTER.

Walter sealed his letter, put the postage stamps upon it, and neatly directed it to his brother, and handed it to the porter to be carried to the post office the next morning; and then, weary and exhausted with the hard day's work, went to his bed and fell asleep.

Chapter XIII.

A DAY IN BELFAST.

BELFAST has been called the "Athens of Ireland," but our friends saw nothing there to indicate that this appellation was well deserved. Only one day could they spend there, and that was to be crowded full of work. Early in the morning, before business men were astir, the whole party left the hotel, and went first to the railway station where the baggage was left, ready to be taken in the afternoon. Reference has already been made to the admirable system for the preservation of small bundles that may be left at the depot. On this occasion, Walter had his carpet bag, raglan, and umbrella, which he tied in one bundle, and paying a halfpenny, or one cent, he gave it to the baggage master, who put upon it a check like this, and gave him a

corresponding ticket, that there might be no mistake about it when he returned. However small or trivial the article, it was carefully placed where the keeper could lay his hand upon it, and as Walter looked into his room he saw that he had a large framework with various compartments, each compartment for articles labelled between certain numbers, and he also noticed that there were hundreds of articles on deposit.

"There are several objects of interest in Belfast, and which shall we take first?" asked Mr. Percy, as they again entered the carriage, after leaving their luggage at the station house.

"I propose," said Mr. Tenant, "that we make a visit to the extensive linen works. I have letters to the proprietors of some of these establishments, and as we have seen none of them, the change may be agreeable."

"Certainly," replied Mr. Percy; "let us go."

"But what do Minnie and Walter say?" asked Mr. Tenant; "we make them equal partners, and give them equal voices with us, on this tour."

"We should acquiesce in your plans, Mr. Tenant, of course, whatever our opinion might be; but preference would lead me the same way with you this morning. I would like to see the mills."

"So should I," added Minnie. "I have seen the mills of Lowell, Lawrence, and Holyoke, and I should like to know if the operatives are as nice looking, well dressed, and well behaved as those in America."

They drove then to the York Street Flax-spinning Company's works, to the proprietors of which Mr. Tenant had letters of introduction. This establishment employs about three hundred men and twelve hundred girls, and they are engaged in the manufacture of Irish linen. These factories are not carried on, as in our country, by corporate companies composed of a large number of small stockholders, but by a few wealthy men, and often by a single individual who has amassed immense wealth.

Walter noticed that the outside of this mill was dingy and dirty, the bricks were of a very poor quality, and covered and begrimed with smoke and coal dust, and looked very different from the bright-red brick factories of our own manufacturing cities. He also called the attention of Minnie to the fact that many of the operatives were very young, mere children, who had been placed at the loom long before they were able to endure the fatigue of a hard day's work.

The inside of the mill was of unfinished brick or stone; the walls, floors, stairs, all of one or the other of these materials; very little woodwork was seen, except in the window frames, the doors, and in the machinery. The floors were oily, the walls covered with dust, and the operatives would bear no comparison with that industrious, cheerful, and intelligent class of our own population. They were very poorly dressed, dirty, and generally barefoot. And yet there were some respects in which the gentlemen thought the establishment excelled those at home; but the children thought the difference was all in favor of our own factories.

Walter was pleased with the huge engine that moved all these spindles, and kept all these men, women, and children employed; and as they stood gazing at it from a little gallery erected for the purpose, the gentleman who conducted them through, asked the children, " How many horse power do you suppose this engine has?"

" Horse power! What is that?" asked Minnie.

" Why," replied the gentleman, " when an engine will do a given amount of work, we say it has so much horse power."

" How is the estimate made?" asked Walter.

" What do you mean?"

" Why, how much is one horse power?"

" Mr. James Watt estimates that ——"

"Who is James Watt?" interrupted Minnie.

"He was a Scotch mathematician, who did much to improve steam engines, and who, though born poor, the son of a tradesman, became a very eminent man, and received high honorary titles from the University of Glasgow, and died in the year 1819."

"But as to the horse power?" queried Walter.

"Yes, as I was saying when the little girl interrupted me, Watt estimates that a horse will raise thirty two thousand pounds one foot per minute."

"Then that is called one horse power."

"Yes."

"And how much power has this engine?"

"How many horse power should you think it was, from the looks of it, and from the work you see it doing?"

"Let me guess," said Minnie.

"Guess is a word we do not use in Ireland; that is a Yankee word."

"Well, I think the engine is about seventy-five horse power."

"What does the young master here think it is?"

"I think it must be more than that," replied Walter; "perhaps about one hundred and twenty-five horse power."

"You both fall below the reality; it is estimated at one hundred and sixty horse power."

"Then this engine would raise, one foot per minute, a weight equal to five million one hundred and twenty thousand pounds."

"Yes, that will answer for a general estimate."

The children were much pleased, and Minnie, as she left the gallery, said, —

"I have a new idea."

"What is it, sis?" asked Walter.

"Why, about this horse power. I never understood it before. I have heard it said that steam engines had such an amount of horse power, but never knew what it meant."

"Where do the operatives live?" asked Walter of his father.

"All about the place, I suppose."

"Do they not have boarding houses, like operatives in our country?"

"No."

"Why not?"

"Because that is not a part of the system."

"That feature of the American manufacturing life," added Mr. Tenant, "is one of the best ideas of our system. Among us, long brick edifices are erected, which have all the outward, and many of the internal, evidences of luxury and ease. Operatives at night are not driven away to rude and wretched tenements, where poverty and filth rule and ruin, or to the den of infamy, or to the street, but have a comfortable *home* provided. Here each girl boards herself where best she can; and consequently many of them scarcely live at all. When they are sick, no care is taken of them; and they die uncared for and unmourned. Vice must be the product of such an arrangement; and we have no reason to be astonished when we are told that many leave the path of rectitude and virtue, and sink into the depth of ruin. One of the wisest and most humane provisions for the comfort and safety of operatives in our American towns is found in the neat, spacious, and even elegant boarding houses, in the kind and maternal care exercised by the women who have the charge of them, and the wise rules which are adopted by the corporations to secure the necessary ends of order and good behavior."

Thus conversing, they reëntered their carriage, and drove from the factory, to visit other objects of interest. And the first place they went to was Queen's College, a finely located structure on high ground, overlooking the city. This college was opened and inaugurated in the year 1849, and is a very creditable institution.

The buildings cost one hundred and fifty thousand dollars, and are quite elegant and imposing in their appearance, being built of red brick, with brown stone facings. The whole structure is six hundred feet long. The library has twelve thousand volumes. The museum of natural history is quite extensive, and its general arrangements are very excellent. It is named in honor of her majesty Queen Victoria, and is very prosperous.

It was vacation time, and Minnie did not see the students. They had gone to their homes, and the old janitor alone received the visitors. This college has a large central tower, and from its top a wide country can be seen. As the party stood there, Minnie asked,—

"What river is that I see, father?"

"The Lagan, my child."

"And what county are we now in?"

"Antrim."

"Is Belfast as large as Dublin?"

"Nearly so; it is the second city in Ireland?"

They stood a long time on this tower, looking out upon the city, which was spread out beautifully before them, and upon the surrounding country, which stretched away into obscure distance.

A DAY IN BELFAST.

As they came down from the tower, Minnie asked Mr. Tenant why the city was called "Belfast." She wanted to know whence the word was derived.

"I do not know," replied Mr. Tenant, "any thing about it; but this little guide book says that the name comes from *Beal-na-far-sad,* which in Irish means the mouth of the ford."

"But where is the ford?"

"Why, the town lies at the confluence of the Lagan and the Belfast Lough."

"Why do you call that sheet of water a 'lough'?"

"That is the Irish name for lake. In Scotland they would call it a 'loch.'"

On leaving the college, the party repaired to the botanical gardens, near by, a charming spot, running down to the banks of the river. Here they saw all the usual things connected with such a place, and spent an hour delightfully in visiting the conservatories, and wandering through the grounds. The taste displayed, the fine scenery, and the delightful views, made the visit a very pleasant one.

Visits to the custom house, museums, cemeteries, and other places of public interest, occupied the day, the last hour of which was spent in a fine ride about the place, from street to street. The ride furnished Mr. Percy a good opportunity to give his children many interesting facts in relation to the history of the city. Walter had many questions which he wished to ask, and Minnie had comments to make on all she saw.

"The first Bible ever printed in Ireland was printed in Belfast," remarked Mr. Tenant.

"When was that?" asked Walter.

"In 1704."

"What is the principal business of the place?"

"The flax spinning is an important branch."

"But are there not other manufactures?"

"Yes, cotton and damask are manufactured here in large quantities."

While Walter was getting at facts in relation to the business and history of Belfast, Minnie was quietly watching the handsome carriages that went dashing by, with drivers having powdered wigs, and footmen with gay velvet coats, and all the appendages of wealth and state.

"Are these the carriages of the nobility?" she asked.

"Yes, of the aristocratic people who live here," replied her father.

"I would like to be an aristocrat," added the little girl, enthusiastically. "There is something so pleasant in the idea of being so rich, having so many servants, and living so easy."

"But some of the nobility of Great Britain are impoverished, and have exhausted their estates, and all that is left to them is an empty title."

"But these here must be wealthy."

"You do not know as the people in these carriages are noble. They may be the wives and children of rich manufacturers, or merchants, many of whom in this country are more wealthy than the titled lords. Besides, having so many servants to take care of, only makes slaves of those who support them. The more simple we live, the more happy we are."

"But men do not think so."

"True, they do not; but it has been proved, conclusively, that many servants and much money only weary and sadden the heart."

"I remember to have read," said Mr. Tenant, "that an ancient queen sent to Alexander the Great, two cooks; but the monarch sent them back, saying he had two cooks that were better than any she could send him; and when he was asked who they were, he replied, *Encrateia* (temperance) and *Askesis* (exercise), and he did not wish to part with them in exchange for those sent by the queen."

The children both laughed, but Minnie did not wish to give up her argument so she added, —

"The ancient ancestry is something honorable at least; and to be connected with people who trace their way back through earls, dukes, and lords, is very ennobling."

"But, Minnie," said Mr. Percy, "you must remember that some of these nobles descended from poor, unlearned people, and their nobility is but a few years old."

"Can you tell me of some such?"

"Yes, I might mention several of the dead and living nobles of England, those who had the largest titles and the most honored names, who descended from a plebeian stock."

"What is *plebeian*?"

"It comes from a Latin word, *plebeius*, and refers to the common people. A plebeian is a common, undistinguished man."

"And now tell me of a case."

"I have one on my mind to the point. In the troublous times of Charles I., a poor, uneducated country girl went to London in search of a place; and after various vicissitudes, hired herself to a wealthy brewer as a 'tub-woman,' to ——"

"Pray what is a tub-woman?"

"A tub-woman is a person in a brewery to

attend to some menial services, just what, I do not know, as I feel little interest is such establishments."

"And what of the woman?"

"For a time she continued at her employment, doing the hard work, when her master, wanting a house servant, and being pleased with her neat, tidy appearance, took her into the family. He had no wife, and after observing the good behavior of this girl, he married her. Soon after the marriage he died, leaving his fortune to his widow. This fortune was very large, and the heir-by-will, wanting some one to settle the estate and counsel with her, applied to Edward Hyde, an eminent lawyer, and retained him for this purpose. Hyde saw that the widow was young, fair, and rich, proposed himself to her in marriage, and became her husband. They had born unto them a daughter, Anne, who privately married the Duke of York, brother to Charles II. Of this marriage came two daughters, Mary and Anne, both of whom ascended the British throne; so that the mother of the wife of James II., and the grandmother of Mary and Anne, queens of England, was only a tub-woman in a London brewery."

"But, pa, this case is an extreme one."

"Perhaps so, dear, but it illustrates the fact

with which I started, that trace ancestry back, and sooner or later it will be lost in an inglorious obscurity."

"And yet the people take much pride in their ancestry."

"Certainly they do; and wherever you go in England, you will see evidences of this. You will see engraved shields and crests, coats of arms, and all the insignia of an illustrious parentage."

"We never see these things at home; why not?"

"Because our institutions do not tend to foster such a pride. We take men for what they are worth, not for what their sires or grandsires were worth."

"This is doubtless so; and yet there is something so imposing in the English aristocracy that one cannot help being pleased with it."

"True, and the nearer you get to the throne, the more you will see of this."

This and similar conversation occupied the time of a long ride about Belfast, and as evening drew near, the whole company repaired, after securing their baggage, to the pier where they were to embark for Scotland.

Chapter XIV.

Farewell to Ireland.

"THE Royal Mail Steamer Elk: seven o'clock," was on a placard hanging against the side of a beautiful steamer that rode easily at the pier in Belfast.

"There she is, Minnie," shouted Walter.

"There *who* is?"

"Why, the steamer that is to take us over to Scotland."

They found it to be so, and at once deposited their carpet bags in their state rooms, and then took their seats on deck among a large company of people, who were, like themselves, about to cross the Channel.

They had not been looking long before they saw several drays roll up to the vessel, and an immense quantity of nice butter and fresh eggs were brought on board. For an hour several strong men were tumbling the firkins and boxes on board, until tons of butter had been freighted. The butter looked very yellow and rich, and

Minnie declared she could make a supper of that alone, without bread.

The eggs came on in baskets, and the children tried to estimate the number of dozens, but could not do it. They were large, clean, beautiful looking eggs, and were very suggestive to our travellers, who had not yet taken tea.

"Where are these going?" asked Walter of a good-natured looking Irishman, who was putting them away.

"They go to Glasgow."

"Your country must be very productive to furnish such quantities of butter and eggs to Scotland."

"This is but a very small part of what we send away."

"I presume not."

"You see," remarked the man, "those steamers lying all along the dock?"

"Yes, sir."

"Well, they are all loading with butter, cheese, eggs, and vegetables, to be carried out to-night. Some of these steamers go to Glasgow, some to Liverpool, and some to other places."

"Do they all carry things produced in Ireland?"

"Yes, and similar steamers go from Dublin,

FAREWELL TO IRELAND.

Cork, and other Irish ports, all laden with the produce of Ireland."

"Certainly, a country that can spare so much for her neighbors ought never to know any thing like want."

"That is just the trouble; the poor people of Ireland produce, and our richer neighbors eat. Ireland starves, while rich landholders send away the products of the soil."

It was not long before Minnie discovered a large drove of cattle, sheep, and swine approaching the steamer; and when they arrived, plank was laid from the wharf to the vessel, and the whole herd, bellowing, bleating, and squealing, was driven into the fore part of the steamer. As they ran, and jumped over, and pushed each other, the children were much amused with their frightened looks and singular appearance. Soon Walter found a practical farmer, who told him all about these cattle, their peculiar habits and races, in which he was much interested. He also met on board Mr. Howland, a neighbor of his father's, the editor of an agricultural paper in Boston, who was on his way to Scotland for the purpose of procuring cattle for propagation in this country. This gentleman entered at once into Walter's views, and being an accomplished and intelligent man, Walter derived from him much valuable information on subjects connected with agricultural life, in which he was interested; and an hour or two, until the steamer started, was passed very pleasantly.

The steamer did not start promptly at the time, but when she did, she rode out upon the river in gallant style.

The Lagan was covered with boats, some with oars and some with sails, some huge and unwieldy, some tiny and graceful, but all filled with men and women enjoying themselves in the closing day. Just below the city, which faded gradually from sight, they saw a sad spectacle. Several boats were dragging the river for a dead body. A lad had been drowned, and on the bank stood a crowd of friends, and just at the water's edge, with her hair dishevelled, her countenance distorted with grief, stood his mother. Just as the Elk, with her happy company, went by, one of the grappling irons fastened in the clothes of the dead lad, and the children saw the men draw him into one of the boats, while the shrieks of his mother at the sight resounded far and wide over the waters. It was, indeed, a mournful spectacle, and a sadness spread over the passengers as they conversed about it.

They left the Lagan, and were out upon the

FAREWELL TO IRELAND. 243

Lough of Belfast. Several other steamers were in sight, and until dark the scene was exhilarating and exciting. Sometimes the Elk was ahead, and sometimes the others left her behind, and the passengers entered into the race with much enthusiasm.

When the night came on, and darkness prevailed, our party went down into the saloon, where they were quite alone until the servants began to spread the table for supper. A light, fancy meal was served, which was hastily swallowed by the passengers, who rushed on deck at its conclusion, leaving Mr. Percy, the children, and Mr. Tenant conversing together. Walter soon got out his writing materials, and began to make his record of the day's labors.

"Father," he said, "I want some facts in relation to Belfast. Can you give me any?"

"What facts, my son?"

"Any that it would be well for me to remember."

"Well, let me think; there has not been a bank suspension here for a hundred years."

"That is a good one — any other?"

"The first newspaper published in Belfast was in 1787."

"Do you know the name?"

"The Belfast News Letter."

"Any other fact?"

"There are thirty-five steam mills for the manufacture of linen, and they employ about twenty thousand hands."

"How many are employed in the whole of Ulster?"

"About three hundred thousand."

"And how much do they make?"

"The whole value of the linen goods manufactured in Ulster is about twenty millions of dollars."

"Well, I have got that written down."

"Some other facts I will give you at another time; and now Minnie can retire, while you, my son, write a while."

Minnie went to her state room, while Walter wrote on; and we give a few extracts from his journal: —

IRISH SEA, 1859.

I sit writing in the cabin of a steamer on the Irish Sea. The night has deepened over the waves, and we have left the shores of Ireland to return no more. I have often heard the country we have been visiting called by various names — sometimes Hibernia, sometimes Erin, and sometimes by other names. I have been trying to find out what these names mean, and I have found out. I find that Hibernia was the ancient name of Ireland, given to it by Julius Cæsar, and borne by it for a long time. I think that Hibernia now would be a much prettier name than Ireland.

I do not wonder the Irish entertain so much affection for their native country. The hills are so green, the valleys so beautiful, the rivers so free and joyous, that I do not wonder that the inhabitants look back with veneration and love to these old familiar scenes. I have travelled up and down the land from Shandon Steeple to Giant's Causeway, and find much more comfort and intelligence than I expected, though the people are not like those in dear New England.

We have had many pleasing incidents, one or two of which I must make a matter of record. One day, when we were in Drogheda, we met an old lady who had a donkey and some baskets. In one of the baskets were specimens of fruit, which she was selling. Her assortment was very small and very poor, and father told her so.

"O, we poor people cannot get what we would like to sell; so we get what we can," she said.

"But what have you in the other basket?" asked father.

"My things."

Father picked out a few oranges, and some other fruit, and just as he was paying her for it, a great, rude lad came along with a dray, and ran roughly against the donkey, almost knocked him over, and completely overturned the baskets.

A cry of terror arose from the woman, and a shrill, piercing shriek from the basket which the woman said contained " my things." Father sprang to the basket, and caught it up, saying, " Hallo! what have you here?"

"O, my poor, dear child — poor boy!" exclaimed the woman, as she caught the basket from father's hand, and took out her child, which was more frightened than hurt, having been so rudely awakened by the fall.

The child was about two years old, and for a few minutes cried most lustily, while the woman made much more fuss than the baby. There soon gathered around us a large crowd of men, women, and boys; some of whom looking on with pity, some inquiring what the matter was, some laughing rudely, and some uttering low remarks and jests.

But at length the baby was picked up, and put into the basket again; the fruit was gathered and replaced; and father gave the woman two or three shillings, which was a sum larger than all her fruit was worth. At first the woman did not seem to comprehend that it was a gift; but after the idea had dawned upon her, that she was indeed to receive all this money, which to her was a very large sum, she was profuse in her thanks, showering her blessings upon us most lavishly.

"God, and all the angels, and all — the — the prophets bless your lordship," she said.

Minnie laughed at the idea of "lordship."

Father replied, "That is blessing enough, good woman," and moved away; but she followed, saying, —

"And may all the saints and martyrs bless you."

"That is enough," persisted pa; "go and sell your fruit now."

But she followed, saying, "The Holy Virgin bless you."

"We don't believe in the Virgin," said Mr. Tenant.

"And sure, sir," she replied, "I don't mean the blessing for you; ye gave me nothing in my trouble."

As she turned away, we all laughed at Mr. Tenant, who had been outwitted by the woman's closing speech, she having bestowed her blessing only where she had been paid for it, as is often the case with people, not only in this land, but in our own.

* * * * *

There was another incident, of a different character, which I must not forget. In the inn at Ballinatoy, where we lodged near the Causeway, Minnie was put into a room occupied generally by the son of the innkeeper. This room was some distance from those occupied by the rest of the party, and was given up to sister because it was more comfortable for a young lady. Minnie retired to rest, and not being tired, soon fell asleep. How long she had slept, she could not tell; but all at once she was awakened by a violent ringing in her room. To her startled ears it did not seem like a natural ringing, but had an unearthly sound. How long it continued she does not know, but it seemed half an hour to her.

"Ding-a-ding, ding-a-ding, ding-a-ding."

"What does it mean?" said Minnie, as the cold sweat started from her forehead.

And still it went, "Ding-a-ding, ding-a-ding."

She raised herself in bed, and tried to discover what part of the room the sound came from. At one time it seemed to be just over her head, and then it seemed to be in another part of the room; now it appeared to be on one side, and then on the other.

"What can it be?" asked Minnie, anxiously, of herself.

"Ding-a-ding, ding-a-ding, ding-a-ding."

"What shall I do?"

"Ding-a-ding, ding-a-ding, ding-a-ding."

While thus the poor girl listened in an agony of suspense, a loud sound was heard, as if a heavy kettle had been dashed upon the floor, and the ringing ceased. All was now still as death, and the ticking of the clock in the room, and Minnie's hard breathing, alone disturbed the solemn silence. For a long time she remained in that state of suspense, then gradually her nerves relaxed, and she fell asleep. When she awoke, broad daylight was flooding the room.

She rose, and at once proceeded to investigate the cause of her alarm. She found a long sheet of iron on the floor beneath the clock, and this was all she could see. At once she repaired to the landlord, who after some little delay was able to explain the whole matter.

It seems that the innkeeper's son wished to rise that morning at an early hour, to go to a town some miles distant, and had set his alarm clock before he gave up his room to Minnie, and forgot to tell her of the fact when the change was made. This was the ringing which she heard, and her fears had produced the impression that the sound came at one time from one quarter, and at one time from another. It also seems that during the day the large sheet of iron had been taken into the room, and stood up carelessly against the wall under the clock; and the running down and hard striking of the clock had so jarred it, that it fell with a crash just as the bell was about through with its striking.

We all concluded that Minnie was a little heroine, not to cry out and alarm the whole house, and we unanimously voted that she should have her own way for a week, which to her was more complimentary than a crown.

* * * * *

O dear, I yawn and gape with weariness; but I must write on a little farther to-night. My eyes are heavy, and I feel more like casting myself into my berth than sitting here; but I will write a little longer, and record the facts and incidents that are in my mind.

* * * * *

To-day, in Belfast, Mr. Tenant wanted to purchase a pocket knife, and the effort to do so developed a little specimen of human nature. We all stepped into a very fine looking cutlery store, and after looking at various styles of penknife, Mr. Tenant selected one, and asked, —

"What is the price of this?"

"Six shillings."

The English shilling is about equal to a quarter of a dollar. Mr. Tenant examined the knife, and thought the price too much, and said so, adding, —

"I will give you five shillings."

The man at once appeared indignant at the idea that it should be supposed he had two prices."

"No, no," he said, "I have only one price; you are in the wrong store to trade in that style."

And then he muttered something about it being impossible to trade with people from America. Mr. Tenant very coolly told him that he could do as he liked about it. The knife was not worth six shillings, and he should not give it; and if the seller did not wish to make a reduction, he could say so, and there was the the end of it. The man made an uncivil reply, again telling Mr. Tenant that he was in the wrong shop for such a trade as that.

We moved to the door, and just as Mr. Tenant was passing out, the shopkeeper called him —

"Come back a moment."

"I think it is no use for us to try to trade."

"I will take off sixpence."

"No, I do not care about purchasing now; your discourteous remarks incline me to go elsewhere."

"I did not mean to offend you; I will let you have the knife for five shillings," said the man, his anxiety to sell increasing as the disposition of Mr. Tenant to buy seemed to fall.

"No, I think not," said the latter; "I offered you five shillings once, and you refused it; now I think I will not trade."

The man still yielded, and finally offered the article for four shillings, saying, "I have some money to raise to-day, and every little helps."

At length Mr. Tenant concluded to buy the knife, so great was the man's earnestness, but paid him for it the five shillings, saying, —

"I know very accurately the value of these knives, and this is worth to me about five shillings. I do not wish to take advantage of your determination to sell, but will pay you the price I originally offered you, though you once refused it. I see you would sell to me at almost any price, but I only wish a fair bargain."

As we left the shop, Mr. Tenant asked me, —

"Walter, have you learned any lesson from

this little transaction between me and this shopkeeper which you have just witnessed?"

"I think I have."

"Have you, Minnie?"

"Yes, sir."

"Well, tell us, Minnie, first, what you have learned."

"I have learned that it is best to beat a man down a little, if you want to get a good trade."

"O Minnie, I am sorry you learned that lesson. I did not design to teach it. But what did Walter learn?" he asked, turning to me.

"I have learned this," I said, "that a man had better say what he means, and not get offended at an offer that he means to take if he cannot get a better one."

"Is that all you have learned?"

"Not all."

"Well, what more?"

"Why, I have learned that it is not right to take advantage of a man's emergencies to get a good bargain. This man wanted to sell his knife; he was determined from the first that you should have it, and you might have secured it for four shillings, which you knew to be less than it was worth. But you gave five shillings, for two reasons, as I suppose."

"What do you think those reasons were?"

"First, you believed the knife to be worth that sum; and second, you had once offered it, and did not feel that you could recede with honor."

"You are right, Walter," added Mr. Tenant.

* * * * *

But I can write no longer. Farewell, Ireland, green isle, sleeping now in the bosom of the sea, — farewell.

Walter folded his paper, wiped his pen, closed up his inkstand, and taking up his portfolio, went to his state room, which adjoined that occupied by Minnie. As he passed her door, which had been left open to admit the air, he paused, and a soft, musical voice from within said, —

"Walter, is that you?"

"Yes, sis, it is, and nobody else."

"Come in, Walter, a minute; I cannot get asleep. What o'clock is it?"

"It is near midnight. But why are you so wakeful?"

"I have been thinking of home, Walter, — of dear mamma and little Charlie, — and as I have thought, my fancy has been working, and I am nervous."

"Well, go to sleep."

"How can I?"

"I do not know; but I have heard it said that a person who is wakeful at night can, by counting one or two hundred backward, so break up the chain of thoughts, and turn the mind from its reflections, that sleep will overpower the faculties."

"I will try it. Good night, Walter."

"Good night, Minnie; may you have happy dreams."

Walter entered his own room, and closing the door softly, bowed down, and committed himself, his father, Minnie, and Mr. Tenant to the kind care of our wise heavenly Father; then he breathed out a gentle prayer for the dear ones at home; and then, repeating the simple, yet sublime, petition given us by Christ, and long ago taught him by his mother, "Our Father, who art in heaven," he went into his berth, and was soon asleep, midway between Ireland and Scotland.

www.ingramcontent.com/pod-product-compliance
Lightning Source LLC
Chambersburg PA
CBHW031730230426
43669CB00007B/311